RESTIOS
OF THE FYNBOS

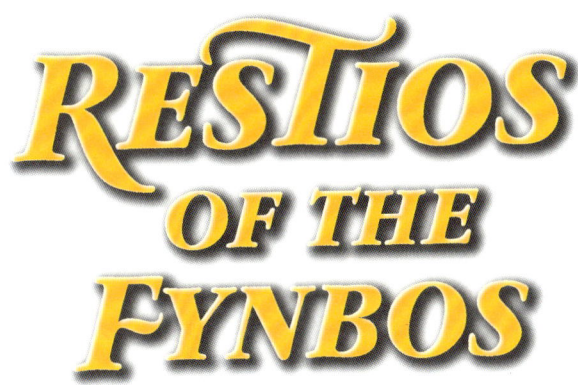

RESTIOS OF THE FYNBOS

ELS DORRAT HAAKSMA
H. PETER LINDER

PUBLISHED BY
THE BOTANICAL SOCIETY OF SOUTH AFRICA

To Eric, Nancy and Alec
E.D.H

First edition, first impression 2000
Botanical Society of South Africa
Cape Town

© *Copyright:*
Published work Els Dorrat Haaksma and Botanical Society jointly
Text Els Dorrat Haaksma pp. 20-184, H. Peter Linder pp. 2-19
Scanned images Els Dorrat Haaksma
Photographs Els Dorrat Haaksma pp. ii; Anne Bean pp. 163-173, 177;
Peter Linder pp. iv, 1-17, 25, 26, 27, 45, 160, 162, 179;
Neville Brown p. 175

Design and layout Els Dorrat Haaksma
Cover design and lettering Andrew van der Merwe

Typesetting, reproduction, printing and binding
Creda Communications, Epping, Western Cape

All rights reserved. No part of this publication may be reproduced,
stored in a retrieval system or transmitted in any form or by any means,
electronic, mechanical, photocopying, recording or otherwise,
without the permission of the copyright owners.

ISBN 1-874999-21-X

Foreword

Cape reeds, biesies, dekriet, or just plain restios – these are some of the common names that have been applied to South African members of the family Restionaceae. Restios form one of the most important structural components of the heathland vegetation, or fynbos of Southern Africa, as it is commonly known, yet to many people they remain an enigmatic, rather intimidating group of plants with the reputation of being difficult if not impossible to identify. The fact that even professional botanists struggle to get to grips with their taxonomy only compounds this intractable image. To the uninitiated, even matching males and females of the same species can be fraught with difficulty.

There are some 480 species of Restionaceae globally, occurring mainly in southern hemisphere countries. Of these about 330 are found in the Cape Floristic Region, so it is clear that this region in particular has experienced a massive radiation of species. Despite this considerable local diversity and their ubiquitous presence in the fynbos, restios have been conspicuously absent from most botanical field guides in this country. But there is a growing awareness of restios, especially among gardeners who have discovered the virtues of some of the larger, more ornamental species in water-wise gardening.

Here at last is a guide that focuses exclusively on the Restionaceae and, moreover, sets out to demystify the classification of these floristically important, strangely beautiful plants. For almost two decades the Publications Committee of the Botanical Society of South Africa has been active in producing regional Wild Flower Guides, each focusing on a specific geographical region within South Africa. *Restios of the Fynbos* by Els Dorrat Haaksma and Peter Linder breaks with this tradition in both content and format by concentrating on a single plant family, providing easy to follow visual aids to identifying the African genera of this fascinating group. Furthermore, the method of production used in this publication is, to the best of our knowledge, unique, as the images reproduced here are obtained by directly scanning live specimens instead of using photographic transparencies, conventionally employed as an intermediate stage in colour printing. The resulting illustrations have exceptional depth, clarity and sharpness. We feel certain that the innovative design and completely new production approach will provide an accessible general introduction to this long neglected but vital component of the Cape fynbos.

J.P Rourke
Chairman, Publications Committee, Botanical Society of South Africa

Acknowledgements
by Els Dorrat Haaksma

When I arrived in Cape Town twelve years ago I had never heard of, or seen a restio plant. But this changed as soon as I met Peter Linder in the Botany Department of the University of Cape Town. I still remember the day he took me to a patch of fynbos and introduced me enthusiastically to his magical world of restios. To me, at first glance, they looked a rather unappealing group of plants whose successful identification, at the time needed for my cytology research project, seemed nothing short of a miracle. However, these plants have a strange habit of 'growing on you' and before I knew it I was totally hooked . . .

This field guide was born out of my fascination, admiration and love for these unique plants and my sincere wish to share this with everyone else who would like to get to know and enjoy discovering the restios.

I would like to acknowledge the following people who have all played a significant role in bringing this book to fruition:

First of all my most sincere thanks to Peter Linder for his immediate and enthusiastic response when I first suggested my ideas for this book, and the co-operation and ready support he subsequently gave me. His vast and unique knowledge of the restios, his constructive comments on my text, his superb photographs, and writing the section 'introducing restios' have all contributed much to this book.

The 3-D scanner at Creda Communications, introduced to me by Stephen le Roux, was surely designed and 'born' for the restios. I am truly grateful for the wonderful co-operation, enthusiasm and skills displayed by Linda Eyden for scanning and retouching and Nicolette Bergstedt for her patience in typesetting what must have been an impossible text and layout. How I shall miss not working with them all anymore.

I am much indebted to the Botanical Society Publications Committee. Whilst they ventured into a completely new kind of guide with this book, they gave me unlimited time for developing ideas and glorious freedom for the design. Grateful thanks also go to John Rourke, chairman of the committee, for writing the foreword.
I thank them all for their trust and hope that this book justifies their faith in me.

I owe Anne Bean special thanks for all the time and effort she spent proof-reading the manuscript many times over. Her comments on the text were invaluable, as were her continued enthusiasm and the moral support she always gave me. My warm thanks to her also for providing such fine photographs for the horticultural section.

For the section on 'Growing restios' I am very grateful to Hanneke Jamieson for generously sharing her horticultural expertise, and for her helpful comments on the early drafts of this section. Thanks also to Hanneke for the use of plant material from her beautiful restio garden at Kirstenbosch.

Anthony Hitchcock too is thanked for his useful comments on the horticultural section.

Pat Lorber, curator of the Bolus and Guthrie Herbaria in the Botany Department of U.C.T. kindly allowed me to use the Herbaria. Deon Hignett from Cape Nature Conservation and Owen Witteridge from the Cape Peninsula National Park provided me with permits to collect restios from the fynbos for the illustrations. My appreciation to them all for their willing co-operation.

Birga Thomas, who, as she says 'has been in books her whole life' guided me in the intricate world of typeface, fonts, headings, leadings and the like.
My special thanks to Birga for her ready helpfulness and great expertise.

Other friends who gave me assistance were members of 'Friends of the Cape of Good Hope Nature Reserve' who tested the educational pages and the Key to the Genera. Their willing help was much appreciated.

Inge Semple made some exquisite watercolour illustrations intended for this book. I thank her for so gracefully accepting my choice of the scanning technology over her art.

I am grateful to calligrapher, Andrew van der Merwe, for his expertise and enthusiastic co-operation in designing the book cover.

Last, but not least, my very special thanks to my daughter Nancy not only for her excellent comments on the text but just as much for her love and support and unfaltering patience with a mother whose only topic of conversation over the last three years was 'the book'. I now look forward to enjoying her company and sharing other interests again.

# By Peter Linder

First and foremost I would like to thank Els Dorrat Haaksma for suggesting the idea of a popular guide to the Restionaceae. Els worked at her plans and soon managed to convince everybody that it was a feasible project, especially after she had seen the new 3-D scanner at Creda Communications and recognised its potential for scanning live restio plants.

The superb 3-D images with which she came back from Creda Communications were so convincing that the Botanical Society Publications Committee offered to include the book in its publications programme.

Els put a tremendous amount of work into the design of the book. I do not know how many times she rewrote and rearranged the text and illustrations in striving for the best designed book to satisfy the needs of tourists, hikers, and amateur as well as professional botanists.

I would also like to thank those who over the years have walked with me in the mountains in the heat of summer, or crunching in snow in winter, looking for restios, particularly Wendy and Anthony Hitchcock and Rachel and Rod Saunders.

But in particular I would like to thank Elsie Esterhuysen, who shared her enormous knowledge of the Restionaceae with me.

Elegia capensis

Contents

Foreword	v
Acknowledgements	vii
INTRODUCING RESTIOS Biogeography, ecology, biology, restios and people, phylogeny and classification	1
IDENTIFYING RESTIOS	20
GRASSES, SEDGES and RESTIOS	22
RESTIO MORPHOLOGY Growth form and rhizomes, culms, sheaths, inflorescences, spikelets, flowers, nuts and capsules	25
KEY to the AFRICAN GENERA	42
GENERA and SPECIES Illustrated species of all African Genera, with keys to all Cape Peninsula species	45
GROWING RESTIOS Introduction, planting, maintenance, list of available species, propagation	161
Glossary	178
Bibliography	180
Names of illustrated species in the morphology section	181
Index	182

xi

INTRODUCING RESTIOS

Whilst many plant families contribute to the wealth of the fynbos, the presence of the Restionaceae is the unique distinguishing feature

Biogeography

The Restionaceae, or as they are commonly called, the restios, is a family of perennial, evergreen, grass-like plants. They range from 10 cm to 3 m in height and often have a tufted growth form. The plants have erect, green, photosynthetic stems, with leaves which are reduced to leaf sheaths. The flowers are very small and contained in spikelets, which in turn make up the flower heads or inflorescences. The family is dioecious, i.e. the male and female flowers are borne on separate plants, and are wind pollinated. The fruit is a nut or capsule.

The Restionaceae is a typical 'southern' or 'austral' plant family. It is found on all the southern continents, with ca.330 species in Africa, ca.150 species in Australia, four species in New Zealand, a single species in South America and a single species widespread in South East Asia.

However, only in the Cape Floristic Region of South Africa do Restionaceae dominate the vegetation over large areas. With so many species and such ecological dominance, the family is obviously of great importance, and this leads to an interest in its biology, ecology and origins.

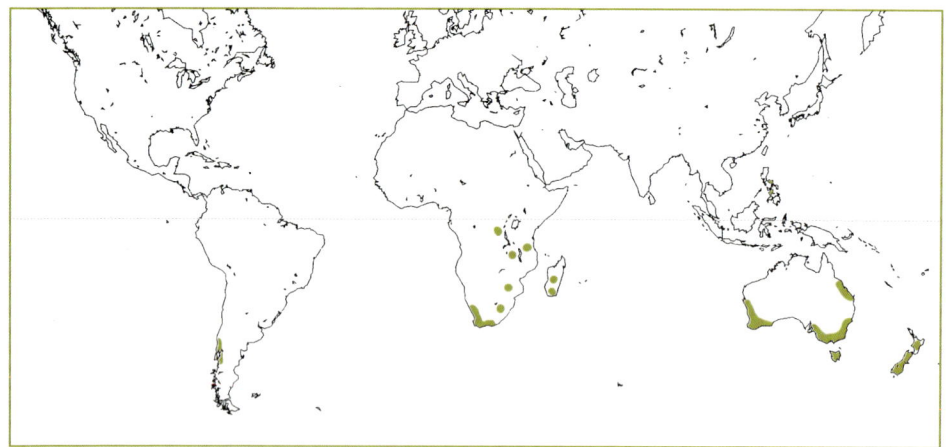

Global distribution (green marked areas) of the Restionaceae

The distribution range over all the southern continents has led to suggestions that the family is ancient, dating to the end of the Cretaceous period, more than sixty million years ago, when the southern continents were still in close proximity to each other, forming the supercontinent Gondwana – a hypothesis supported by fossil pollen records from southern Africa.

introducing restios

> ## FYNBOS
>
> Fynbos is the dominant vegetation in the Cape Floristic Region. The word comes from the Dutch 'fijn bosch' which described the narrow-leaved bushes characterizing much of this vegetation. However fynbos also supports broad-leaved bushes, for example members of the Proteaceae family. The ca. 8000 fynbos species can be divided into several groups, according to their growth form. One of these is the restioid group including the family Restionaceae. Whilst any of the other groups can be absent from a particular habitat, the family of the Restionaceae forms the unique distinguishing part of fynbos.

The hypothesis is that at this time the family would have been widespread on all the southern continents, and when the continents became separated each drifted off with its own complement of Restionaceae. However, another possibility is that the family crossed the Pacific Ocean only recently (in the last thirty million years) leading to the establishment of the single South American species, *Apodasmia chilensis*. This species is very closely related to a species in New Zealand, which is found under very similar ecological conditions, strengthening this hypothesis.

The distribution of the Restionaceae in Africa is very uneven. There is a single species in Madagascar, which is also found in the Democratic Republic of the Congo, Tanzania and Malawi. Another species is found on the Chimanimani mountains of eastern Zimbabwe. In South Africa there are four species in the Natal Drakensberg, one of which is also found in the Northern Province and Mpumalanga. But the vast majority of the species are found in the fynbos of the Cape Floristic Region, especially on the hard sandstone mountains of the south-western and southern Cape.

The distribution of individual species varies from widespread, like *Ischyrolepis sieberi,* which ranges from the Richtersveld to Port Elizabeth, to narrowly endemic species, restricted to single mountain peaks, like *Hypodiscus montanus* from Misty Point behind Swellendam.

The greatest richness in species is found in the Kogelberg mountains, where over one third of all Restionaceae species are found. Moving away from the Kogelberg, the species richness drops off, until one reaches the peripheries of the Cape Floristic Region, where there are rather few species. This distribution pattern is typical for most elements of the 'Cape Flora', and is seen in *Erica,* Proteaceae, *Disa* (Orchidaceae), and numerous other groups.

Ecology

Restios can be found in virtually all habitats of the fynbos, from sandy plains to mountain summits and from very dry places to seasonally wet or permanent marshes. In many areas the Restionaceae often make up the most dominant component of the fynbos vegetation to the extent that they are regarded as the 'loyal supporting cast' to the other more colourful flowering families such as Ericaceae, Proteaceae and Iridaceae.

However they cannot be found as annuals or in aquatic habitats and are also absent from the forest understorey. **Ischyrolepis subverticellata** and **Restio fourcadei** are often found along the margins of the forests or in the light shade of scrub forest along stream margins, but avoid the deep shade of the forest.

Restionaceae are excellent indicators of the ecology of an area, and if the list of Restionaceae for a particular spot is known, it is possible to predict the climate and soil moisture conditions.

Mountain fynbos in the Slanghoek Mountains with **Elegia amoena**

introducing restios

Seasonally inundated flats at Cape Point, with Elegia cuspidata *and* Elegia filacea *forming extensive monospecific stands*

Chondropetalum microcarpum *in coastal dune vegetation at De Hoop. Coastal sand restios typically spread by underground rhizomes, forming mats*

Seepage vegetation on Table Mountain, with hummocks of Anthochortus crinalis

Sandy plains in the Slanghoek mountains with large stands of Elegia spathacea

A seepage on the Hexberg, Bokkeveld mountains, with Elegia grandispicata *fringing the wet centre of the seepage*

An ice-encased restio on Groot Winterhoek near Tulbagh

Biology

The Restionaceae have a rich biology. Although this will be discussed under a number of different headings, these processes are all integrated to make a functional plant that successfully traps pollen of the right type, sets seed which is effectively dispersed, and germinates successfully to grow into an adult plant. The interactions with the physical environment and with the animals and other plants which share their habitat provide yet another interesting aspect of the biology of the Restionaceae.

POLLINATION

All Restionaceae are wind pollinated, and although this means that there are no interesting visible interactions between pollinators and the flowers, the way the flowers and inflorescences are adapted for wind pollination is particularly fascinating.

Restionaceae are dioecious, i.e. male and female flowers are borne on separate plants. This may function primarily in preventing the plants from fertilizing themselves, but at the same time has led to morphological specialization of the different roles of male and female flowers.

A variety of restio flowers

The flowers are very small and inconspicuous. The petals and sepals are dull brown, sometimes transparent and scale-like. This suggests that their main function is to protect the anthers and ovary. There are no nectaries. The flowers are aggregated into small spikelets, which in turn make up the inflorescences. Although the role of the spikelets, as such, for wind pollination is not quite clear, the numbers of spikelets per inflorescence will certainly affect pollination.

introducing restios

Male spikelets of Hypodiscus willdenowia

Male flowers, to be efficient at wind pollination, have to produce large amounts of pollen, which have to be shed into the wind. The large pollen production is achieved by numerous flowers with three anthers each, rather than few flowers with many anthers. In addition, the anthers are quite large and, when ripe, bright yellow and very visible. Most species have the anthers on long filaments protruding from the bracts and exposing the anthers outside the spikelet to the airflow.

As usual, there are exceptions, and in the *Elegia-Chondropetalum* group of genera the ripe anthers open inside the petals. However the petals open to release the pollen.

Male flowers of Chondropetalum tectorum *with anthers inside the petals and pollen dusted all over, x 5*

Electron microscope scan of pollen of Hypodiscus striatus *with the typically rounded aperture, x 1000*

The pollen also has to be modified for efficient transport by air. The most important feature is that the pollen is not sticky (unlike that of insect-pollinated plants), thus ensuring that it is dispersed like dust in the wind. In addition the grains are round and smooth, which appears to improve their aerodynamic characteristics.

POLLINATION (continued)

Female flowers show some spectacular adaptations to wind pollination. These are evident in the construction of the inflorescences and in the shape of the styles, both designed to maximize the ability of the flowers to trap pollen.

The styles, as in the grasses, are usually feathery and in most species exposed outside the spikelets, where they are well positioned to filter the pollen out of the air. They are found in a variety of beautiful colours, from white to pink or red or even maroon. Some species have quite substantial, stiff styles.

Female spikelets of **Restio quinquefarius**

In the genera ***Staberoha*** and ***Elegia*** the bracts and spathes are much enlarged and completely enclose the flowers and even whole spikelets. In these plants the bracts and spathes presumably act as air-scoops, which funnel the wind past the styles, or cause local eddies resulting in the pollen dropping down onto the styles. These mechanisms are amazingly efficient, as very little 'foreign' pollen has been observed on these styles. The plants appear to trap only their own pollen, excluding the pollen from other species and the general debris that is found in the air.

More detailed information on flowers, spikelets and inflorescences can be found in the morphology section.

Spathes of **Elegia** *sp. enclosing the spikelets*

Stout styles of **Ceratocaryum argenteum** *partially hidden by the big spathes*

introducing restios

DISPERSAL

Seeds from a variety of restio species

Restionaceae have a remarkable diversity of seed dispersal mechanisms, and these are intricately linked to the construction of the flowers. In the simplest, and presumably the primitive method, the ovary of the flower produces two or three small seeds and the fruit is a capsule. When the seeds are ripe, the capsule splits open, and the seeds are released. The seeds are generally of similar shape, more or less elliptical, and 1-2 mm long. However, there is great variation in the ornamentation of the seed surfaces, from completely smooth and shiny, to pitted, ridged, or otherwise modified. This ornamentation can best be seen under a magnification of x 10 or more. The purpose of the ornamentation is obscure, but a clue may be found when looking for the seed on the sand around the base of the plant: it is almost invisible. The seed is the same size as sandgrains, and the texture and shape mimics the sandgrains. So possibly this is a way of camouflage. How the seeds are dispersed from the parent plant is not quite clear, as there are no obvious dispersal agents.

Seeds, x 5

In the species in which only a single seed is formed in each ovary, the fruit is a nut or nutlet, and a diversity of dispersal mechanisms has developed. In these cases the seed stays inside the nut, and often the petals and sepals persist around the nut, aiding its dispersal. For many small-nutted species no obvious additional dispersal mechanisms exist. However, in some species of *Staberoha* and *Calopsis* and in all species of *Thamnochortus* the lateral sepals are deeply keeled, forming a wing around the nut, thus forming a wind-dispersed fruit. This is very evident in *Thamnochortus*, where the winged nutlet can be seen blowing along in the wind.

Winged nutlets of Thamnochortus lucens, *x 3.5*

DISPERSAL (continued)

The most interesting dispersal mechanism is found in species of *Willdenowia, Hypodiscus, Mastersiella, Ceratocaryum* and *Cannomois,* where the nuts are evidently dispersed by ants. These nuts are much larger than those of the other genera, up to 10 mm long. The walls are very hard, distinctly woody and brown to black in colour. The persistent petals and sepals are papery, often much smaller than the nut, forming a small skirt around the base of the nut. As the nut ripens the stalk at the base of the nut becomes swollen and fleshy, and contains oils which are apparently very attractive to ants. This structure is called an elaiosome and stays attached to the nut. Once the nuts have dropped to the ground ants carry them away underground and feast on the elaiosomes. This interesting dispersal mechanism protects the seed from predators like mice, as well as from fire.

A few species in this group of genera make very large nuts, ca.11 mm in diameter but have no elaiosomes to attract the ants. However the seedlings of these plants all come up from several centimeters below the soil, so something buries the nuts. Currently suspicion falls on mice that might hoard the nuts but then fail to find their buried stores, or are themselves killed before they can retrieve them.

In general plants involved in this kind of dispersal mechanism make few spikelets, each one carrying only one big nut. So there appears to be a close link between the dispersal mechanism, nut size, the architecture of the spikelets and the inflorescences of the plants.

Nut of Willdenowia glomerata, *x 3.5*

elaiosome

Nut of Hypodiscus aristatus, *x 3.5*

introducing restios

GERMINATION

The 'seed' (seeds, nuts and nutlets) in the wild germinates directly after the onset of the winter rains. The seedlings then have a short 'window' period of about four months during which to establish themselves before the harsh summer starts, in which they have to survive severe drought and searing temperatures at ground level.

There appear to be two germination patterns:
Plants with seeds and nutlets make small seedlings but make large numbers of them. Presumably these have an extensive mortality in the first summer, although there is no data on this.
Plants with nuts make seedlings which grow very rapidly and quickly make deep taproots, which can reach deeper into the soil for moisture during the summer months. Although these plants produce much less 'seed', the seedlings obviously have a better chance of survival.

During their first year the seedlings look very different from the adult plants and have numerous finely-branched sterile culms. This bushy sterile growth probably maximizes photosynthesis.
In the second winter a new set of culms is made, usually still with the seedling morphology, and the first year's growth dies back. Only in the third year do the plants reach the typical 'adult' morphology without the finely-branched culms. These new adult culms terminate in inflorescences which set seed.

Seedling of a species of restio, *with the seedcoat lifted above the ground by the leaf-like, green cotyledon*

There is no information on how long adult plants live. There are some indications, largely from the cultivated plants at Kirstenbosch, that their life-expectancy may be quite variable. For example ***Restio festuciformis,*** is short-lived (two years), while ***Chondropetalum tectorum*** and ***Thamnochortus insignis*** are known to live over ten years.

ANIMAL INTERACTIONS

Superficially it appears as if Restionaceae have little interaction with animals. For most plant families the most striking plant-animal interaction concerns pollination biology, and since Restionaceae are wind pollinated, there is no such interaction here.

The second interaction usually concerns seed dispersal and apart from ants carrying away the large nuts (see Dispersal p. 9) there appears to be little in this area either.

However, there is extensive 'hidden' interaction: Chrysomelid bugs are pervasive pollen predators on the male plants of the Restionaceae. There are several bug species involved in this, but they appear to be unselective as to the Restionaceae which they attack. Whole populations of a species have been observed where virtually all the pollen has been eaten by the bugs before it is released. They tear open the bracts and tepals and devour the pollen in the anthers.

A Chrysomelid bug on Restio bifidus

Leafhoppers of the tribe Cephalelini are highly cryptic sap-suckers, which are totally restricted to a few species of Restionaceae and spend their whole lifecycle within one plant. They insert their mouthparts into the culms, reaching the sap inside the plants. Fortunately the plants do not appear to suffer much damage from this. The bugs are very difficult to see as they are shaped like the leafsheaths of the Restionaceae.

In addition, there are many other bugs that live on Restionaceae, and are camouflaged like the various organs of the Restionaceae. It is not clear what they are doing on the plants, but considering the antiquity of the Restionaceae, this evidence could be reflecting a long evolutionary association. It would be fascinating to find out more about these Restionaceae-insect associations.

Restionaceae are often grazed. Possibly the most widespread grazer is the vleirat, **Otomys**. The rats fell the culms of the Restionaceae, then cut them into shorter lengths, and eat the softer tissue above the nodes. In older vegetation one can often find the middens of these animals: small piles of neatly chopped restio culms. In some cases there is a path leading from the nest of the vleirats to their favourite eating places, where extensive middens can be found.

introducing restios

Dassies *(Hyrax)* will also graze Restionaceae, especially the plants resprouting after fire, and one can often see extensive areas of closely cropped restios near dassie colonies. It is likely that restios are also eaten by klipspringer *(Oreotragus)* antelope. The extent and impact of this grazing is not known.

Collecting bugs on **Rhodocoma** capensis

Some Restionaceae, especially *Willdenowia incurvata,* are eaten by cattle.

The biggest impact of grazing is possibly on the seed of the Restionaceae. Nothing much is known about the fate of the small loosely dispersed seed, but the bigger ant-dispersed nuts, when not buried by ants, are bitten through and the contents eaten. This might have been the most potent force in driving the evolution towards ant-dispersal.

Elegia filacea *grazed by* **Otomys**

FIRE

Surviving–or exploiting–fire is one of the dominant themes in the ecology of plants from the fynbos. In a simplistic sense there are two possible responses: either the plants are killed by fire and then re-establish from seed, or the plants survive as stems or underground rhizomes and resprout from these. Following either of these two strategies can have far-reaching effects on the biology and ecology of the plants.

Plants which can resprout after fire often have rhizomes and larger underground structures in which they store some of their photosynthetic product. These extra food resources are used for very rapid growth directly after the fire, so resprouting plants will quickly regain their full photosynthetic capacity after fire.
But the 'cost' of diverting and storing resources underground usually results in new plants with smaller inflorescences, fewer flowers and a lower seed output than their reseeding relatives.

Reseeding plants, by contrast, have slow initial growth rates from the seed, and it may take two to three years before they are mature enough to produce flowers. However, over the longer term these species usually grow taller, have much larger inflorescences, and set much more seed than the resprouters.

Ecologically, resprouting plants often occur scattered in the landscape, while reseeders commonly form dense stands. This may be the result of the massive recruitment of reseeding plants that happens after fire. However, two fires within too short a timespan can lead to the complete loss of the reseeding plants, as not enough time has elapsed between the consecutive fire-events to allow the plants to set sufficient seed for the post-fire re-establishment of the next generation. One often finds mountain slopes totally dominated by resprouting species, suggesting that an inappropriate fire event in the recent past has led to the local extinction of the reseeding Restionaceae species.

Classifying Restionaceae into reseeders and resprouters is still incomplete but initial surveys suggest that the proportions may well be half-and-half.

introducing restios

An Anthochortus crinalis *marsh in the Slanghoek mountains a few months after fire. The species is being re-established by prolific seed germination (the fine lawn-like appearance is due to thousands of seedlings)*

The remains of a tussock of Cannomois nitida, *killed by fire and unable to resprout*

Restios and people

Restionaceae were probably used as building materials by people long before the first European settlement in the Cape. Examples of the use of **Cannomois taylori** as roofing material, as well as for the walls of huts can be seen in the Wupperthal and Moedverloor areas. In the Sandveld there is still some remnant knowledge of the use of Restionaceae for house construction and a typical 'reed' house made up of five different species of local Restionaceae can still be seen in Hopefield.

Cottages at Moedverloor constructed almost entirely from **Cannomois taylori**

During the time of the Dutch East India Company in the Cape, thatching was mostly done with **Chondropetalum tectorum,** with a 'reed cutter' collecting and preparing the thatch. The use of Restionaceae as roofing material has persisted through the centuries, with **Thamnochortus insignis** the most used species nowadays, because of its excellent long culms.

Currently there is a big trade in 'thatching reeds' (mostly **Thamnochortus insignis,** but to a lesser extent also **T. erectus),** from the coastal areas from Albertinia to Bredasdorp. These reeds are almost exclusively used for thatching, but are still entirely collected from the wild.

A rough shelter built from **Cannomois taylori***, near Eselsfontein in the Cederberg*

A broom made of a **Willdenowia** *species*

16

introducing restios

Thamnochortus insignis *being harvested in the Albertinia area*

Bundles of T. insignis *(stacks of 500 or 1000 bundles) in the Albertinia area, drying in preparation for being sold*

There is as yet no attempt to cultivate the thatch commercially, but veld-management is effectively being used to enhance the production of the material. The reeds are variously prepared and marketed, and are even exported in small volumes. Roofs thatched with high-quality thatch are reputed to last for more than fifty years before they need to be redone.

Other domestic uses of Restionaccae are relatively minor. There is a local production of brooms from whatever restio species in the area appears to be suitable, and a small amount is used in the dried flower industry.

And the final product – a roof being thatched

However there is a rapidly growing horticultural demand for the family. Many species form striking plants, and have a low-maintenance, water-efficient character. Hence they are ideal for areas in which periodic water-shortages may make water-demanding gardens unacceptable. This is dealt with in more detail in the section on growing restios (p. 161).

A cottage at Darling built out of several kinds of restios and plastered, known as a typical 'riethuis'

17

Phylogeny and classification

Restionaceae are related to the grasses and sedges. Superficially the plants from these three families look very similar, and detailed investigations have revealed many more hidden characters which indicate the close relationship between the families. However, there are some obvious characteristics by which these families can be distinguished from each other and these are given on p. 22.

The closest relatives of the African Restionaceae are the Australian Restionaceae, and these, in turn, are related to a number of relatively bizzare West Australian genera in other families: *Hopkinsia, Lyginia, Anarthria* and *Ecdeiocolea.*

The Restionaceae comprises 55 genera and ca.490 species, of which 19 genera and ca.330 species are found in the Cape.

There is currently research in progress on the relationships between the genera, and the groups of genera, and it remains possible that there will be some changes in these groups. In addition, there is as yet no formal suprageneric classification for the family as a whole: the existing classification bears no relation to our current understanding of the relationship between the genera, but no new classification has as yet been proposed. The groups are therefore referred to by informal names.

The groups of genera in the African Restionaceae are as follows:
Willdenowia group *(Willdenowia, Hypodiscus, Cannomois, Ceratocaryum, Mastersiella, Nevillea, Hydrophilus, Anthochortus).* This group is characterized by the flowers having two styles and the fruit being a nut or nutlet containing one seed. This group shows specialization towards ant dispersal of the nuts.

Thamnochortus group *(Thamnochortus, Staberoha* and *Rhodocoma).* This group has pendulous male spikelets and long sheaths, the apical portions of which are membranous and decay on older culms. The culms frequently have clusters of sterile branches at the nodes, but are otherwise usually unbranched. In this group the specialization is towards wind dispersal of the nutlets. Although most studies have placed *Staberoha* in an isolated taxonomic position, it is included in this group because of a number of similarities to *Thamnochortus,* especially the pendulous male spikelets and the tendency towards wind dispersal of the nutlets.

Restio group *(Restio, Calopsis, Platycaulos).* In this group the flowers have three styles and, except for *Calopsis* which produces a nutlet, the fruit is a capsule which splits open to release the seeds. The plants rarely have spreading rhizomes.

introducing restios

Ischyrolepis is very distinctive because of its persistent style 'peg' (stylopodium). Although its pollen grains are very different from those of the genus *Restio* its growth form is similar and it also has a capsular fruit. They may, therefore, be closely related.

Elegia group *(Elegia, Chondropetalum, Dovea, Askidiosperma)*. This group is characterized by sheaths which drop off as the flowers mature, leaving very distinctive small abscission rings along the culms. The tepals are rounded and hard. In addition, the bracts are variously modified – in *Elegia, Chondropetalum* and *Dovea* the bracts are smaller than the flowers, and the spikelets are not very distinctive. In *Askidiosperma* the bracts are much longer than the flowers and are membranous, soon becoming frayed. In *Elegia* the fruit is a nutlet, whilst the other genera have capsules, although in many cases this is difficult to observe.

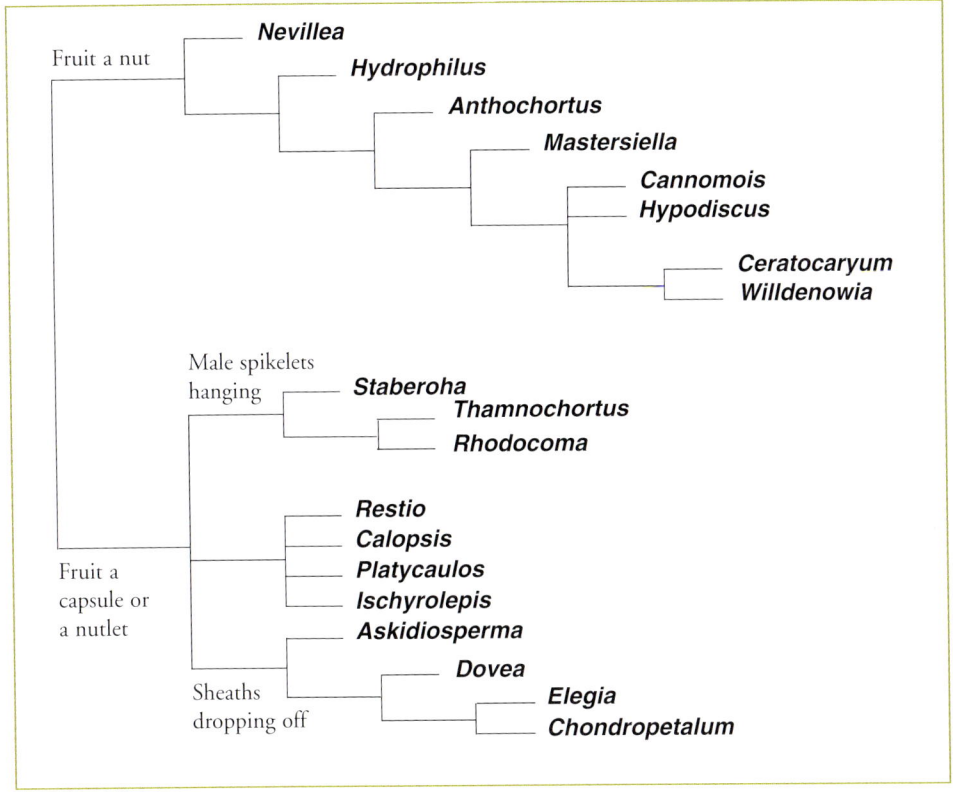

Phylogenetic relationships amongst the Restionaceae

Identifying restios

Identifying restios is exciting, but it is by no means an easy task. So, before you run into the fynbos armed with your magnifying glass, expecting this book to bring instant success, first please spend some time familiarizing yourself with the morphology of the restios and do some 'armchair identification' at home.

Having done your homework, find some friends with lots of patience to join you on your walk in the fynbos, and enjoy the challenge of the restios.

The following four sections will give you information to help you with your identification:

1. GRASSES, SEDGES and RESTIOS, pp. 22-23
The illustrated examples show the overall differences between restios and the other two related and look-alike families.

2. RESTIO MORPHOLOGY, pp. 25-41
This section illustrates and describes in simple terminology the unique botanical characteristics of the Restionaceae. This information will help you to identify the special features of your specimen which you will need to understand sections 3 and 4. All illustrations are **life size,** unless magnification is indicated.

3. KEY to the AFRICAN GENERA, pp. 42-43
This key gives the major distinguishing characteristics of each genus. It is organized in the form of a table so that a quick overview of all the genera can be seen. Identifying the culm and sheath features of your specimen will be the easiest way to start using the key. This will bring you to a group of genera. Having identified the group in this way you will have to look at other characteristics to find the genus of your specimen.

The key can, however, be used in any order, and it will become clear that it is not always necessary to have the specimen in flower. In many cases identification to genus level can be done throughout the year using characteristics other than the flowers, a true bonus of the restios.

Genera which do not occur on the Cape Peninsula are shown in brackets.

identifying restios

4. GENERA and SPECIES, pp. 44-159

This section contains illustrations and descriptions of a selection of species of all African genera.

Each genus is represented by one or more of the most common or attractive species and a species key is given for all genera occurring on the Cape Peninsula.

All species keys are based on the features of female plants unless otherwise indicated.

Male and female plants of the same species are illustrated and described on opposite pages, except when they are identical, or too big. In the latter case they appear on subsequent double pages.

Features common to both male and female plants of a species are grouped together in the text.

All illustrations are **life size,** except for some very small structures, where enlargement enhances the detail and magnification is indicated.

In most cases only the top part of the culms are shown, but the text gives the height and growth form of the whole plant. Habitat and distribution are given for all species.

Grasses ... # Sedges ...

The illustrated examples show the overall differences between the restios

Inflorescence at the tip of the culm

Culm usually hollow

Leaves with blades and leafsheaths at the nodes along the culms

Inflorescence not at the tip of the culm

Culm solid, often triangular

Leaves with blades and leafsheaths

Leaves and leafsheaths usually clustered at the base of the culms

and *Restios*

and the other two related and look-alike families, the grasses and sedges.

Inflorescence at the tip of the culm

Culm mostly solid

Leaves (without blades), with leafsheaths only, at the nodes along the culms; sheaths split down to the base

Leafsheaths persistent or dropping off

— leafsheath

Some Sedge species, like ***Tetraria thermalis*** (Berg palmiet) may look like a Restio, but their leafsheaths are not split, they are like a cylinder around the culm

Culm with abscission rings where the sheaths have dropped off

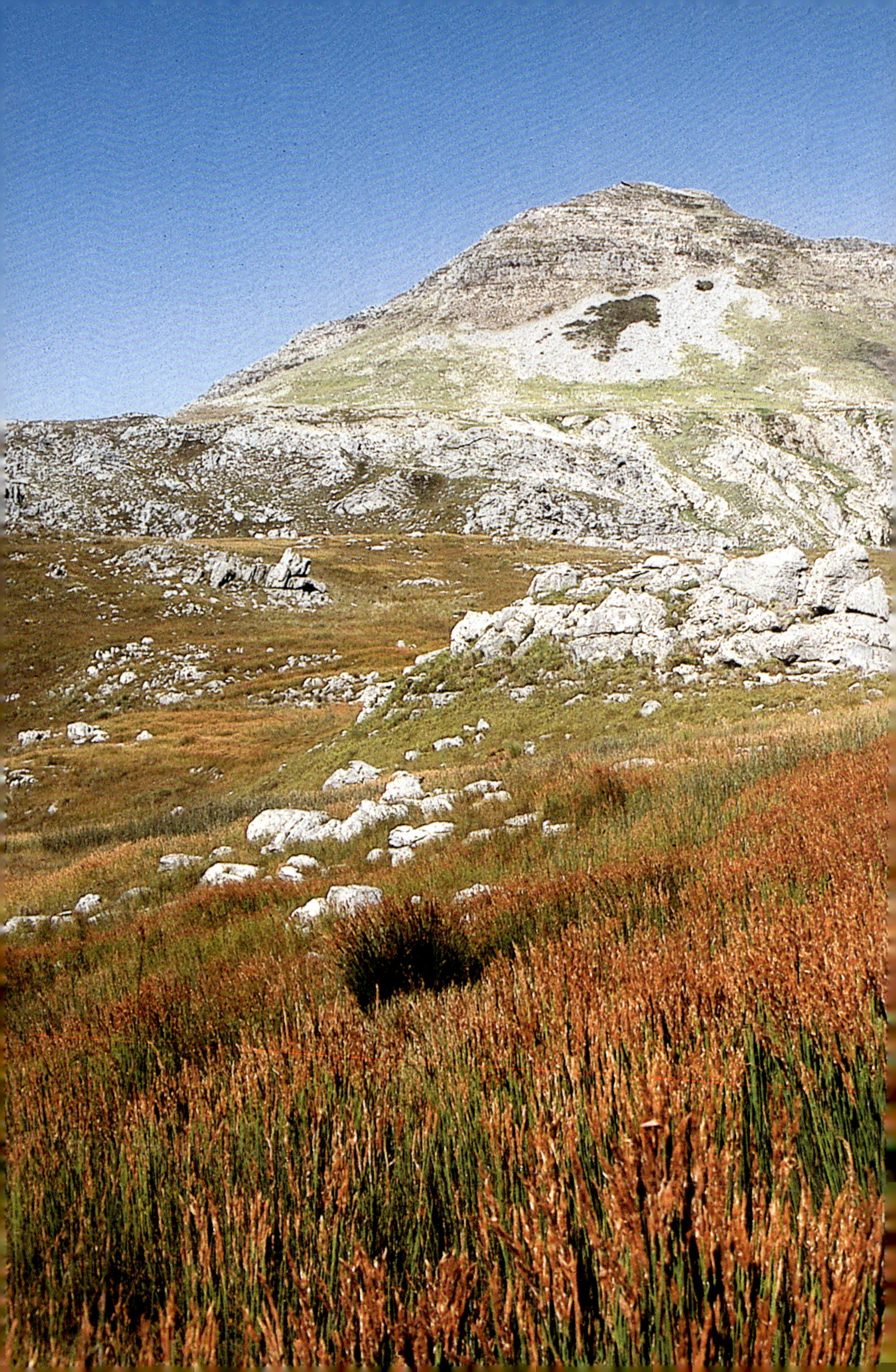

RESTIO MORPHOLOGY

The Restionaceae display an amazing variety of special features

The following pages illustrate and explain in simple terminology these unique botanical characteristics, and aim to encourage and help you towards successful identification

Growth Form

There are broadly four types of growth form (plant shape) amongst the restios:

1. TUFTED PLANTS
These plants have a narrow base and a much wider upper area, i.e. many culms are closely spaced on a short to medium length rhizome.

Chondropetalum ebracteatum

This is the most dominant and characteristic restio growth form in the fynbos. In some species only a few culms arise from the rhizome, branching into a much wider bush, e.g. genus **Willdenowia**.

Hypodiscus aristatus

Elegia racemosa

restio morphology

2. PLANTS with LONG LINES of PARALLEL CULMS

These plants have their culms spaced on long creeping rhizomes (see illustrations on pp. 28-29).

3. TANGLED BUSHES

These plants do not have rhizomes. The branched culms have roots at their culm bases and form either small, low and dense ground cover or taller, floppy (e.g. genus *Mastersiella*) or tangled (e.g. some *Restio* and *Ischyrolepis* species) bushes. The tangled bushes of *Anthochortus crinalis* form big soft hummocks.

small tangled bush

x 0.5

no rhizome

roots

Mastersiella digitata

Anthochortus crinalis

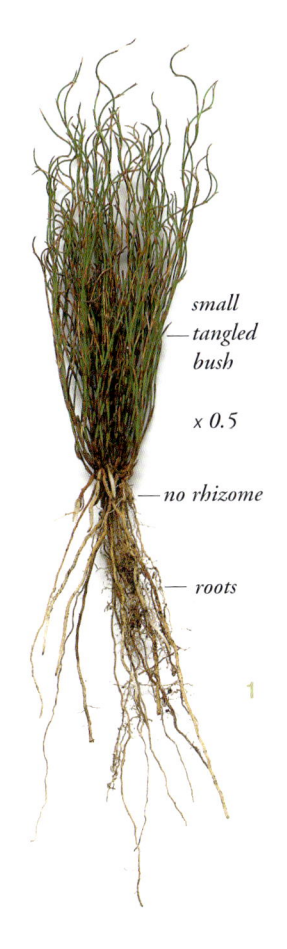

4. TALL RESTIOS

These plants can reach up to 3 m in height, growing on strong spreading rhizomes. The lower part of the culms are often bamboo-like (e.g. *Calopsis paniculata*).

Calopsis paniculata

Rhizomes

Restio plants consist of three main parts, the aerial stems or culms, an underground stem (usually a rhizome) and the roots. The culms are discussed on pp. 30-31.

x 0.5

scales

thick compact rhizome

root

1

culms

rhizome

root

2

x 0.5

A **RHIZOME** can be distinguished from a root by having nodes and internodes (like a stem), which are covered by hard shiny, scale-like leaves. It bears roots and, being perennial, it keeps producing new culms. In many species it will resprout after fire has burned away the aerial culms.

Since both roots and culms are short-lived (at most three years), the rhizome is the organ that gives the plant longevity.

restio morphology

As can be seen from these examples, rhizomes vary in length (from short and compact to long and creeping), diameter and branching pattern.

x 0.5

x 0.5

— very short rhizome

strong, long rhizome with culms in long lines

culms evenly spaced on rhizome

x 0.5

part of thin, long creeping rhizome

The growth form of the aerial part of the plant is closely linked to the size and structure of the rhizome and the way the culms are spaced on it. In some species this is a good diagnostic feature.

• *Names of illustrated species listed on p. 181*

29

Culms

In the Restionaceae the stems are called culms. They are the only parts of the plants which are green and as such, responsible for photosynthesis.

The culms have a variety of features which are easy to recognise and can therefore be used as a first step towards the identification of the genera. They are listed below with the numbers of the illustrations in brackets:

BRANCHING PATTERN
- unbranched (1, 2, 3, 5, 6, 7, 9)
- branched, from sparsely to much branched (8, 10)
- branches clustered in whorls at the nodes along the culm (see p. 62)

SHAPE of the culms
- cylindrical and straight, tapering towards the top (1, 2, 3, 5, 6, 7 9, 10, 11); a few species are hollow (9)
- cylindrical and curved or curly (4)
- flattened (see pp. 92, 158)
- square (4-angled) (8)

SHEATHS
- dropping off (5, 6, 7, 9)
- persistent (1, 2, 3, 4, 8, 10, 11) (see p. 32)

1 2 3 4 5 6 7 8

restio morphology

SURFACE TEXTURE of the culms

a. smooth
b. hairy
c. striped or ridged
d. with warts

a   b   c   d   x 3.5

STERILE CULMS

In many genera young plants and those regenerating after a disturbance, e.g. fire, usually first produce a kind of low bushy growth at the base of the plant.

Similar growth can be produced at the nodes of the main culms or on the branches the year after flowering (11).

Both are small sterile culms, i.e. culms which do not flower. The sheaths of these culms have awns so long that they look like culms themselves.

• Names of illustrated species listed on p. 181

Sheaths

Restios do not have leaves like those of most other flowering plants. Their leaves are reduced to just the (leaf) sheaths. These are always split down to the base (8 a,b,c).
The sheaths occur in two different ways:

SHEATHS PERSISTENT
and showing a spectacular variety of shapes and sizes (1, 2, 5, 8-13)

or

SHEATHS DROPPING OFF
leaving distinct, small, dark abscission rings at the nodes along the culm (3, 4)

Make sure to base your identification on older culms of the plant (those which have flowered) as sheaths are always present on the young culms

1   2   3   4   5   6   7

restio morphology

The following features are often diagnostic of a genus or species

the way the sheaths are
WRAPPED AROUND the CULM e.g.
- tightly (1, 8, 11, 12, 13)
- loosely (2, 5, 6, 7, 9, 10)

SIZE and SHAPE
of the 'body' of the sheaths e.g.
- pointed (1, 5, 6, 7, 8, 9, 11)
- with straight 'shoulders' (2, 10)
- with an awn (1, 2, 7, 8, 9, 10, 11, 12)

SPECIAL MARGINS e.g.
- membranous (2, 7, 10, 11, 12)
- frayed (13)

TEXTURE and COLOUR

Sheath showing split

The sheaths of the culms of male and female plants of the same species are always **identical.** This is a particularly useful feature for matching male and female plants of the same species whose inflorescences are different.

A variety of sheaths

• Names of illustrated species are listed on p. 181

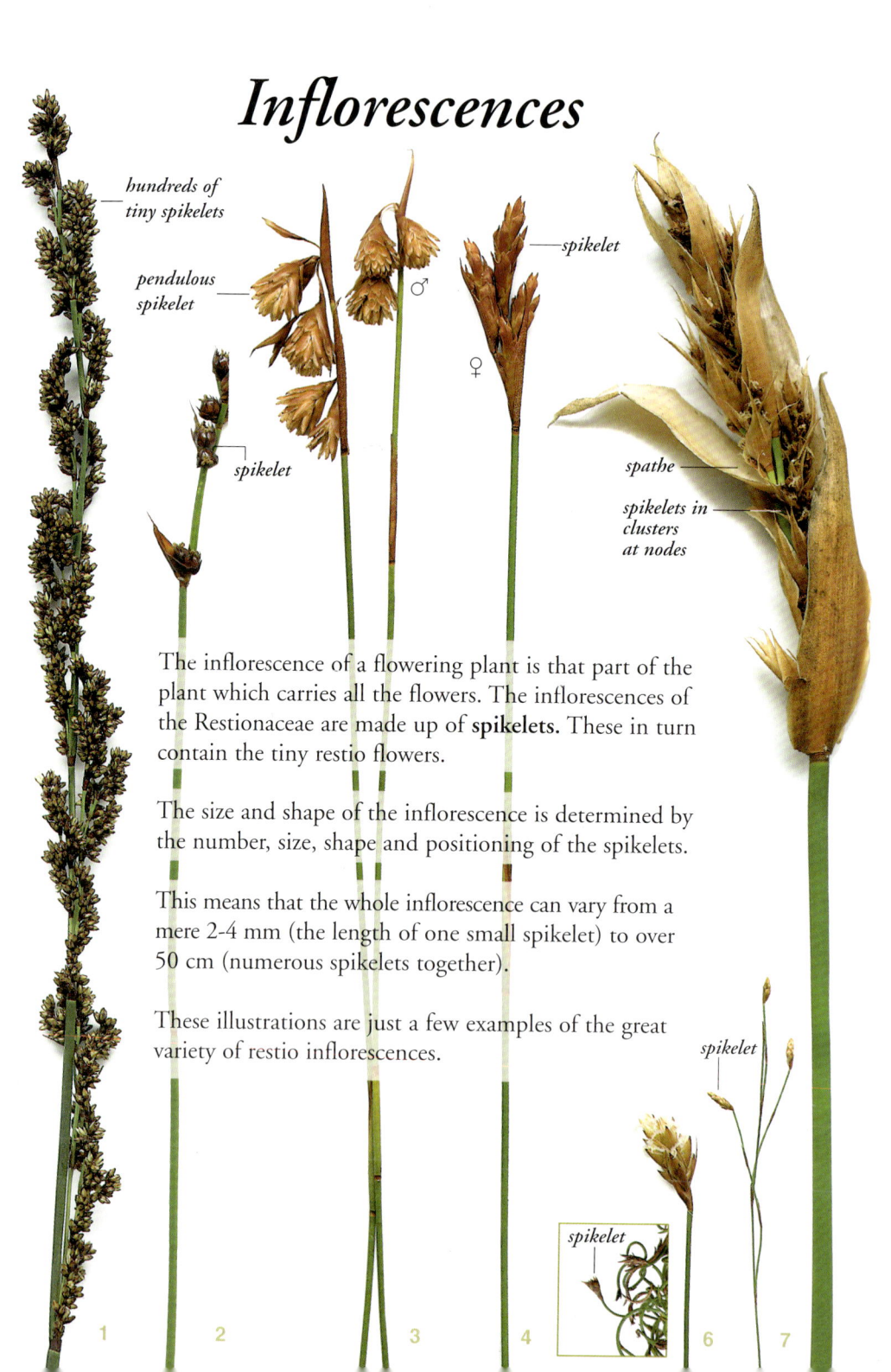

Inflorescences

hundreds of tiny spikelets

pendulous spikelet

spikelet

spikelet

♂

♀

spathe

spikelets in clusters at nodes

The inflorescence of a flowering plant is that part of the plant which carries all the flowers. The inflorescences of the Restionaceae are made up of **spikelets**. These in turn contain the tiny restio flowers.

The size and shape of the inflorescence is determined by the number, size, shape and positioning of the spikelets.

This means that the whole inflorescence can vary from a mere 2-4 mm (the length of one small spikelet) to over 50 cm (numerous spikelets together).

These illustrations are just a few examples of the great variety of restio inflorescences.

spikelet

spikelet

1   2   3   4   5   6   7

restio morphology

♀

♂

pendulous spikelet

RESTIOS ARE DIOECIOUS, which means that each species has its male and female inflorescence on separate plants. They are usually referred to as male and female plants.

MALE and **FEMALE INFLORESCENCES** of the same species are not always similar. In many species they are very different, a feature which is known as sexual dimorphism. Examples of this are shown by illustrations 3, 4 and 12, 13.

In some genera the whole inflorescence or separate parts of the inflorescence are ensheathed or subtended by big bracts called **SPATHES** (8).

9   10   11   12

13

• *Names of illustrated species listed on p. 181*   35

Spikelets

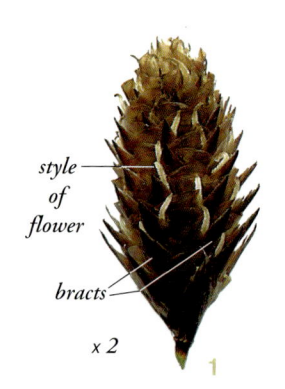

A restio spikelet is a structure which is made up of **bracts** and **flowers.** Each small stalkless flower is seated on a central axis directly above a bract (a modified leaf).

In most spikelets the bracts are bigger than the flowers and only the anthers or styles of the flowers may be visible.

The number, size, shape and texture of the bracts as well as the number of flowers, are different in each species and are important diagnostic features of the species.

style of flower
bracts
x 2
1

tiny spikelets
2
3
4

pointed bracts
5

6
7

NUMBER of BRACTS and FLOWERS

Spikelets can have many bracts, each one with a flower (1, 5, 6, 7) or have many bracts of which only some have a flower (2, 3, 4, 8).

spathe
8

bracts
styles
bract
9
10
11

In some genera the spikelets consist of several bracts (9, 10, 11 12), but only the top bract has a flower (with 2 styles) which usually develops into a nut or nutlet. The other bracts are empty (sterile).

bracts
12

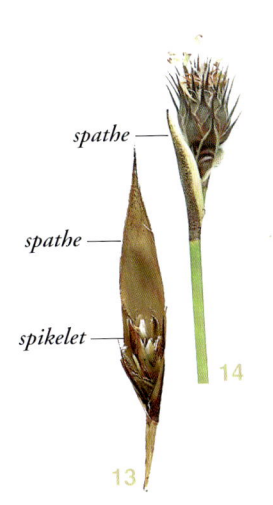

restio morphology

SPATHES
Most spikelets are subtended by a spathe (modified bract), which can vary from small and insignificant to big, overtopping and hiding the spikelets (13, 14, 15, 17).

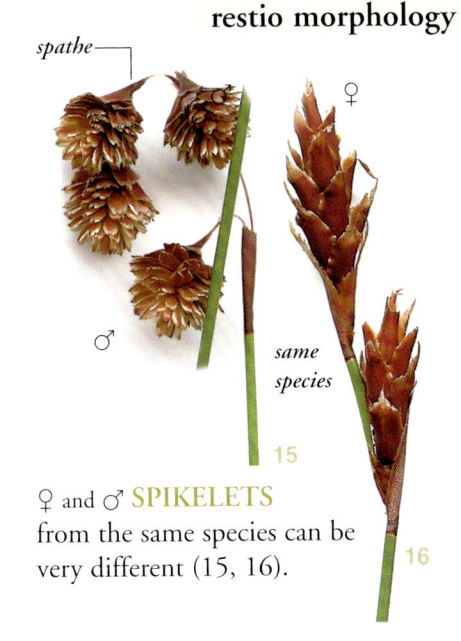

spathe — 14
spathe
spikelet — 13

spathe — 15
♂
same species
♀
16

♀ and ♂ SPIKELETS
from the same species can be very different (15, 16).

spathe — 17
spikelet

18
20 x 5
x 5
♂
bracts — 19
x 5

IRREGULAR SPIKELETS
In some genera the spikelets are poorly organized and do not look like regular spikelets (17, 18, 19, 20).

21
22

SHAPE and TEXTURE of the BRACTS
In some species the bracts are hard and tightly wrapped around the spikelet (21), in others they have long awns (22) or they can be lacerated and look like stiff hairs (23).

23
x 5

• Names of illustrated species listed on p. 181

Flowers

Restios have very small flowers (1-10 mm long) and in most genera one can hardly see them as they are partly hidden by the bracts of the spikelets, only 'visible' by their bright yellow anthers and white, pink to maroon or even green styles.

Female flowers consist of an **ovary**, **styles** and **tepals**, whilst the male flowers have **anthers** and **tepals**.

ANTHERS

These are the reproductive parts of the male flower which produce the pollen. Each male flower has 3 anthers and in most genera the ripe anthers hang out from behind the bracts to disperse the pollen in the air (2, 3, 4, 6, 7, 8).

STYLES

These are the reproductive parts of the female flower which pick up the airborne pollen. There can be 1, 2, or 3 styles per flower, but the number for each species is constant. Their bases can be free or joined and there is much variety in size, texture, shape, and colour (1, 5, 9-15).

restio morphology

TEPALS

Restio flowers have 3 petals and 3 sepals, (arranged in 2 whorls), forming a perianth of 6 tepals. The tepals are usually brown, but their size, shape, and texture vary greatly for each species.

Gently peel away the bracts of the spikelets to expose the flowers. You will need a magnifying glass of at least x 10 to be able to see the features clearly.

x 5 16

17 ♂ x 5

SHAPE and TEXTURE of TEPALS

In the flowers of some species the petals and sepals differ in size (16), whilst in others they are equal, differing in texture and shape, e.g. either hairlike (17), bony and rounded (18), or membranous and flat (19, 20). There is great variety amongst the genera and species.

x 3.5 18

19 — tepals x 5

20 — nut — tepals x 3.5

WINGED and KEELED SEPALS

In some genera 2 sepals have become folded, forming 2 lateral keels or 2 wings. They can be hairy (21, 22) or hairless (23, 24, 25).

21 keel — x 3.5

keel — 22 x 2

23 — wing — nutlet — style x 10

25 — keel x 3.5

24 x 3.5

• *Names of illustrated species listed on p. 181*

Nuts and Capsules

smooth nuts x 3.5

1

In the Restionaceae the ovary of the female flower develops into one of two types of fruit, either a **nut** or a **capsule**, containing the seeds.

In twelve genera the fruit develops into a nut and in seven genera it becomes a capsule (see key on p. 42).

2 nut flattened on one side, x 2

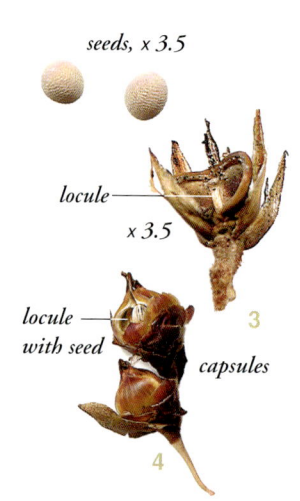

seeds, x 3.5

locule x 3.5

locule with seed

3

capsules

4

CAPSULES

A capsule can hold 1, 2, or 3 **seeds**, but the number for each species is constant; each seed is contained in a separate, small compartment or chamber called a locule. When the seeds are ripe the capsule splits open to release them.

The seeds are 1-2 mm long and vary in shape, colour and surface ornamentation (see also p. 9).

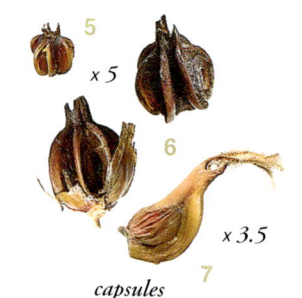

5 x 5

6

x 3.5

7 capsules

x 5

seeds

NUTS

A nut contains only 1 **seed**, which is kept inside the nut during dispersal. Restio nuts can be divided into two types: nuts and nutlets.

9

elaiosomes

8

pitted nuts, x 3.5

11

triangular nutlets enclosed by the perianths, x 5

tepal

elaiosome

10

smooth nut, x 3.5

40

restio morphology

tepals
x 5

bracts

x 3.5

12
nuts with elaiosomes

13

14

NUTS and NUTLETS

The nuts are large, up to 10 mm long, with hard, woody walls and frequently with elaiosomes at their base.

The elaiosomes are a much sought after food by ants and play an important role in dispersal of the nuts. This is discussed under Dispersal on p. 9.

The nutlets are smaller than the big nuts, less than 5 mm long, and with softer walls. They never have elaiosomes.

wing

nutlet

16

flower, x 10

In some genera (e.g. ***Thamnochortus***) the nutlets have a persistent perianth with two winged lateral sepals. It is thought that these aid in wind-dispersal of the nut.

15

x 5

• Names of illustrated species listed on p. 181

41

Key to the African Genera

abscission ring

CULM and SHEATH	GENUS	PAGE
CULMS unbranched SHEATHS dropping off	CHONDROPETALUM ELEGIA ASKIDIOSPERMA	46 54 70
CULMS branched SHEATHS dropping off	[DOVEA]	72

sheath
CULMS unbranched SHEATHS persistent
	THAMNOCHORTUS
	STABEROHA
	RHODOCOMA
	HYPODISCUS
	[CANNOMOIS]
	[NEVILLEA]
	[CERATOCARYUM]
	   Willdenowia (1 sp)
	   Restio (3 spp)
		74
		86
		90
		94
		120
		100
		102
		106
		155

sheath
CULMS branched SHEATHS persistent
	WILLDENOWIA
	MASTERSIELLA
	ANTHOCHORTUS
	[HYDROPHILUS]
	CANNOMOIS
	CALOPSIS
	ISCHYROLEPIS
	RESTIO
	PLATYCAULOS
	   Elegia (3 spp)
	   Thamnochortus (6 spp)
	   Chondropetalum (1 sp)
		104
		108
		110
		114
		116
		122
		128
		144
		158
		65
		85
		52

CULMS with branches in whorls at the nodes along the culms SHEATHS persistent	Elegia capensis [Rhodocoma capensis] [Ischyrolepis subverticellata]	62 92 136

- Take care to base your identification on the persistence or absence of sheaths on older culms of the plant i.e those which have flowers, as in all species sheaths are always present on the young culms
- Young sheaths are usually green before they mature into their brown colours

key to the genera

No. of STYLES per flower	FRUIT	SPECIAL FEATURES
3	capsule	inflor. brown-black, spathes dropping off, bracts < flowers
3	nutlet	inflor. 'golden', spathes persistent
3	capsule	bracts transparent, hairlike, > flowers
3	capsule	flowers and capsules large, round, and black seeds white
1	nutlet	♂ spik. oblong, PENDULOUS, top half of sheaths frayed
2-3	nutlet	♂ spik. bell-shaped, PENDULOUS
3	capsule	♂ spik. oblong, PENDULOUS, top half of sheaths frayed
2	nut	♂, ♀ spik. spindle-shaped, bracts very spiky
2	nut	nuts flattened on one side
2	nutlet	♂ spik. cone-like, bracts rounded, hard
2	nut	♂ bracts and tepals white
2	nut	same as for WILLDENOWIA
3	capsule	same as for RESTIO
2	nut	sheaths bi-coloured, top part transparent
2	nutlet	♂ spik. cone-like; nutlet black, shiny
2	nutlet	spathes and sheaths with long hairlike awns
2	nutlet	bracts papery, silvery, shiny
2	nut	nuts flattened on one side
3	nutlet	in many aspects similar to the genus *Restio*
2	capsule	ovary (capsule) with persistent stylopodium (peg)
3	capsule	species very diverse
3	capsule	culms flattened, with mostly GREEN SHEATHS
2	nutlet	same as for ELEGIA
1	nutlet	same as for THAMNOCHORTUS
2	capsule	same as for CHONDROPETALUM
3	nutlet	many spik. in big inflor. at tip of culm
3	capsule	spik. at tips of numerous short branches
2	capsule	spik. at tips of branches; capsules with persistent stylopodium

Abbreviations
- *inflor.* inflorescence
- *spik.* spikelets
- *sp* species (1)
- *spp* many species (>1)
- ♂ male
- ♀ female
- [ ] indicates genera or species not found on the Cape Peninsula
- > indicates bigger than
- < indicates smaller than
- indented genera (in lower case) have their major number of species in another group

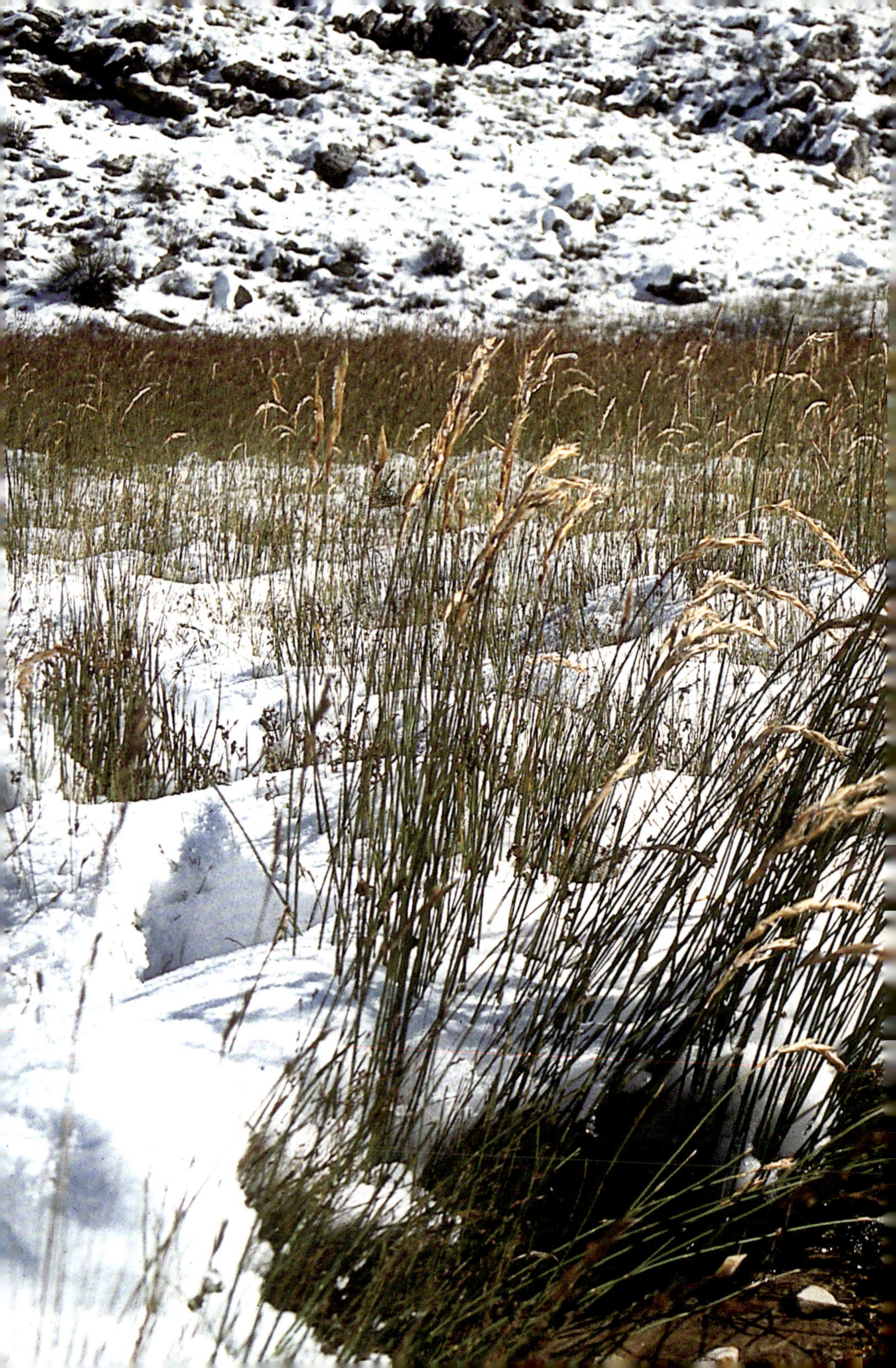

GENERA AND SPECIES

...turn the following pages and discover the magical world of restios ...

Chondropetalum
C. tectorum

Male plant

INFLORESCENCE
numerous spikelets, clustered in groups at the nodes, forming a loose, deep brown to black spiral around the axis; spathes soon dropping off

spikelet, x 5

spikelets very small, poorly defined, ripe anthers not protruding from the flowers, pollen released inside the bony tepals

bracts bony, shorter than the flowers

Male and Female plants

CULMS unbranched

SHEATHS dropping off, leaving small, distinct, dark abscission rings at the nodes along the culms

GROWTH FORM plants tufted on a short rhizome, varying in height from 30 cm to 1.5 m

HABITAT widespread, common in seasonally wet areas often forming very extensive stands, mainly on coastal forelands

Chondropetalum

Female plant

There is much variation in size of plants and inflorescences. This illustration is from a much smaller plant than that of the male plant opposite.

INFLORESCENCE spathes, **spikelets** and **bracts** like those of the male

FLOWERS
- *perianth* tepals bony, deep brown to black, petals longer than sepals, all 6 tepals similar in shape

- *styles* 3, feathery

- *fruit* a CAPSULE, 3-chambered, with ornamented seeds

spikelet, x 5

Chondropetalum tectorum, *also called 'dak riet' (roof reed) was one of the main thatching reeds used during the occupation of the Western Cape by the Dutch East India Company. At present most thatching is done with* **Thamnochortus insignis** *from the southern Cape as it has much longer culms.*

Chondropetalum
C. ebracteatum

Male plant

INFLORESCENCE many spikelets, often at right angles to the culm, clustered in groups at the nodes, forming a loose deep brown to black spiral around the axis; small spathes soon dropping off

spikelets poorly defined, ripe anthers not protruding from the flowers, pollen released inside the tepals

bracts shorter than the flowers

Male and Female plants

CULMS unbranched

SHEATHS dropping off, leaving small, distinct, dark abscission rings at the nodes along the culms

GROWTH FORM plants tufted on a very short rhizome, varying in height from 30 cm to 1 m

HABITAT sandstone, at all altitudes and particularly common on the shallow soils of Table Mountain

Chondropetalum

Female plant

INFLORESCENCE several spikelets clustered in groups at the nodes, forming a loose, deep brown to black spiral around the axis

spikelets poorly defined, bigger than those of the male

bracts and spathes like the male

FLOWERS round
- *perianth* tepals bony, deep brown to black, very shiny, all 6 similar in shape; petals as long as the sepals

- *styles* 3, feathery

- *fruit* a CAPSULE, 3-chambered

flower, x 5

young culms with the sheaths still on

Chondropetalum
C. mucronatum

Male plant

INFLORESCENCE hundreds of spikelets on branchlets clustered at the nodes along the inflorescence, with big 5-10 cm long spathes, which eventually drop off

Male and Female plants

CULMS unbranched, stout, erect, up to 10 mm in diameter

SHEATHS dropping off, leaving small, distinct, dark abscission rings at the nodes along the culms

GROWTH FORM a stout plant growing on a strong rhizome, up to 1.5 m in height; culms flowering soon after they emerge from the ground, and seeds shed just before the culms reach their full height

Chondropetalum

spathe

young culms with sheaths still on

Female plant

INFLORESCENCE
several spikelets clustered at each node, hidden by big, 5-10 cm long spathes, which eventually drop off

spikelets poorly defined

bracts shorter than the flowers

FLOWERS round
• *perianth* tepals bony, deep brown, and shiny, all 6 similar in shape; petals as long as the sepals

• *styles* 3, brushlike

• *fruit* a CAPSULE, 3-chambered, with ornamented seeds

HABITAT
plants forming extensive populations, often much taller than the surrounding vegetation, in seeps on sandstone plateaux of mountains which receive south-east cloud in summer; plants are killed by fire, but re-establish from seed

Chondropetalum

CULMS	PETALS, SEPALS and BRACTS mature to a deep brown to black colour		
CULMS unbranched		FLOWERS < 3 mm petals as long as the sepals	PLANTS with slender culms, on long rhizomes
		x 5 x 5 FLOWERS < 3 mm petals longer than the sepals	PETALS rough with a distinct middle ridge
		x 5	PETALS smooth or rough on upper half, with a slight middle ridge
SHEATHS dropping off		x 3.5 FLOWERS > 3.5 mm petals as long as the sepals	SPATHES 5-10 cm long, hiding the spikelets
		x 3.5	SPATHES < 5 cm long CULMS slender
CULMS unbranched, with only one persistent sheath		FLOWERS < 3 mm petals longer than the sepals	
CULMS branched, with persistent sheaths		FLOWERS < 3 mm and with 2 styles x 3.5	PLANTS growing in tufts on long deep-seated rhizomes

52

Chondropetalum

7 Peninsula species, 10 species in total

C. rectum	HABITAT clayey, gravelly or sandy soils, in wet or marshy areas DISTRIBUTION coastal forelands from Bredasdorp to Malmesbury and near Wolseley in the Worcester Valley	
C. nudum	HABITAT marshy areas DISTRIBUTION sandy coastal forelands from Darling to Albertinia	
C. tectorum	HABITAT marshy areas DISTRIBUTION coastal forelands from Clanwilliam to Grahamstown	
C. mucronatum	HABITAT swampy soil in the mountains DISTRIBUTION from Bainskloof to the Cape Peninsula and on to Riversdale	
C. ebracteatum	HABITAT shallow sand over rock or deeper soils on well drained mountain slopes and plateaux DISTRIBUTION from the Slanghoek Mountains to the Cape Peninsula and to Riversdale	
C. deustum	HABITAT shallow sand over rock or peaty soils in seasonally wet areas DISTRIBUTION on the Cape Peninsula and along the mountains between Jonkershoek and Betty's Bay, as far east as Bredasdorp	
C. microcarpum	HABITAT dunes and coastal limestone outcrops DISTRIBUTION from Melkbosstrand to Port Elizabeth	

flowers

C. nudum

• *Species in shaded blocks are fully illustrated on pp. 46, 48, 50*

Elegia
E. filacea

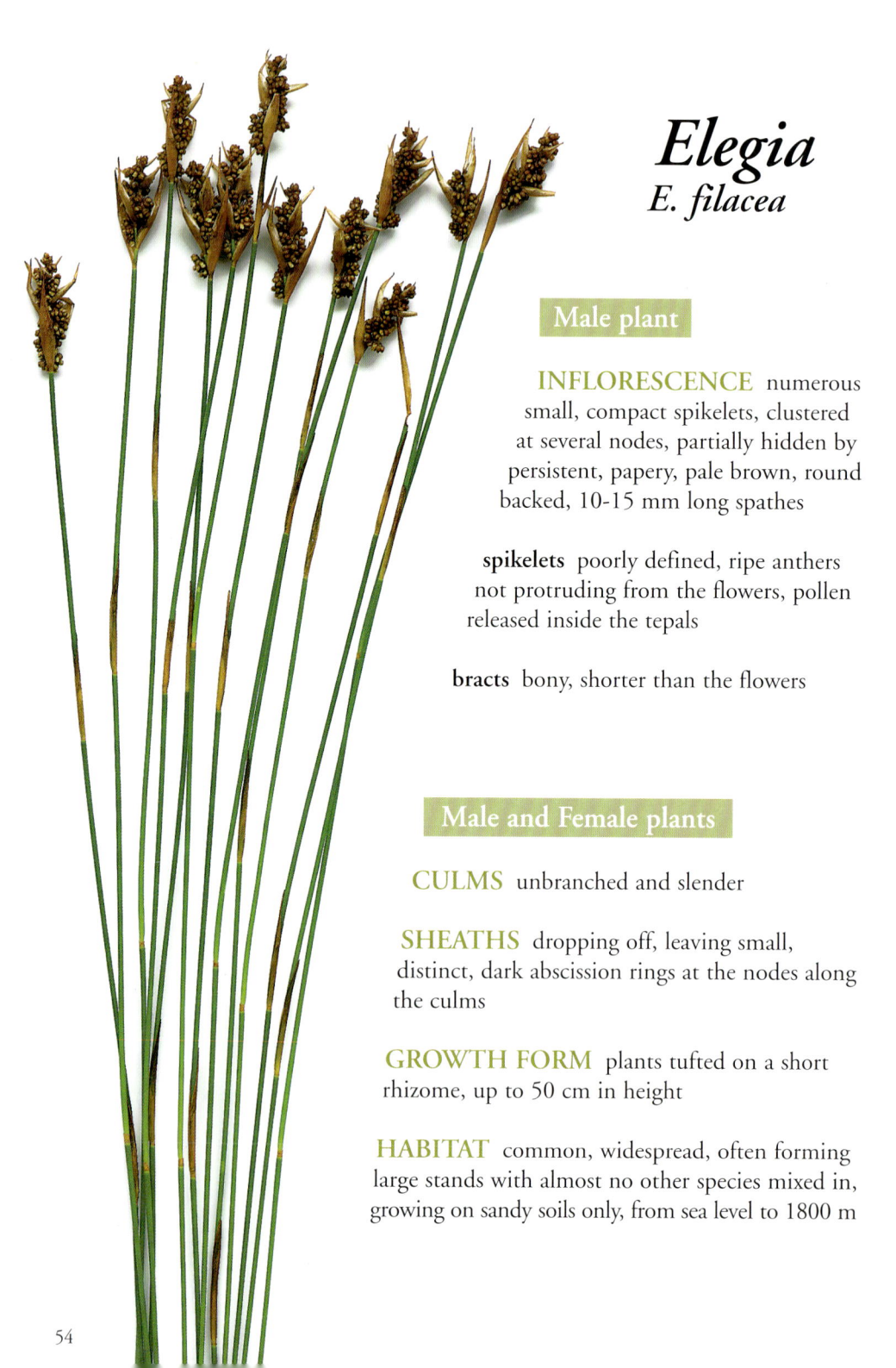

Male plant

INFLORESCENCE numerous small, compact spikelets, clustered at several nodes, partially hidden by persistent, papery, pale brown, round backed, 10-15 mm long spathes

spikelets poorly defined, ripe anthers not protruding from the flowers, pollen released inside the tepals

bracts bony, shorter than the flowers

Male and Female plants

CULMS unbranched and slender

SHEATHS dropping off, leaving small, distinct, dark abscission rings at the nodes along the culms

GROWTH FORM plants tufted on a short rhizome, up to 50 cm in height

HABITAT common, widespread, often forming large stands with almost no other species mixed in, growing on sandy soils only, from sea level to 1800 m

Elegia

spathe

Female plant

INFLORESCENCE numerous small, compact spikelets clustered at several nodes with spathes slightly bigger than the male and almost completely hiding the spikelets

spikelets and **bracts** like the male

flowers, x 5

spikelet, x 5

FLOWERS

- *perianth* tepals woody, like the bracts, but longer

- *styles* 3, brushlike, short, lying flat on the ovary

- *fruit* a NUTLET, triangular

55

Elegia
E. stipularis

Young plant with flowers still in bud

Plant just before flowering

Elegia

♂ *Flowering plant*

♀ *Flowering plant*

E. stipularis resembles *E. filacea* in the inflorescence (see pp. 54-55), but differs in having branched culms and persistent sheaths, forming dense tussocks up to 50 cm in height; note the spectacular colour changes of the maturing inflorescences

Elegia
E. fenestrata

young inflorescence still in bud

inflorescences just before flowering

spathe

Elegia

spathellae

inflorescences in flower

This is an example of a group of **Elegia** *species which are all at least 50 cm in height, or have culms which are at least 1.25 mm in diameter (see species key, p. 69)*

Male and Female plants

INFLORESCENCES similar, with big spathes and much smaller spathellae, partly hiding the spikelets;
these pages illustrate the development of the inflorescence

CULMS unbranched

SHEATHS dropping off, leaving small, distinct, dark abscission rings at the nodes along the culms

GROWTH FORM culms growing straight and parallel on a spreading rhizome

HABITAT coastal sand, in seepages or along streams, below 100 m

Elegia

spathe with spikelet

spikelet, × 2

E. cuspidata

E. racemosa

E. fistulosa

hollow culm

Elegia

INFLORESCENCES OF 5 DIFFERENT SPECIES

These illustrations show inflorescences of 5 different **Elegia** *species, which are all at least 50 cm in height or have culms which are at least 1.25 mm in diameter*

Male and Female plants

INFLORESCENCES usually similar, with the big persistent spathes often characteristic of the species

CULMS unbranched

SHEATHS dropping off, leaving small, distinct, dark abscission rings at the nodes along the culms

GROWTH FORM varies according to the species

For more detailed information on these tall species consult the **Elegia** *species key, p. 69*

E. intermedia

E. persistens
(off Peninsula)

61

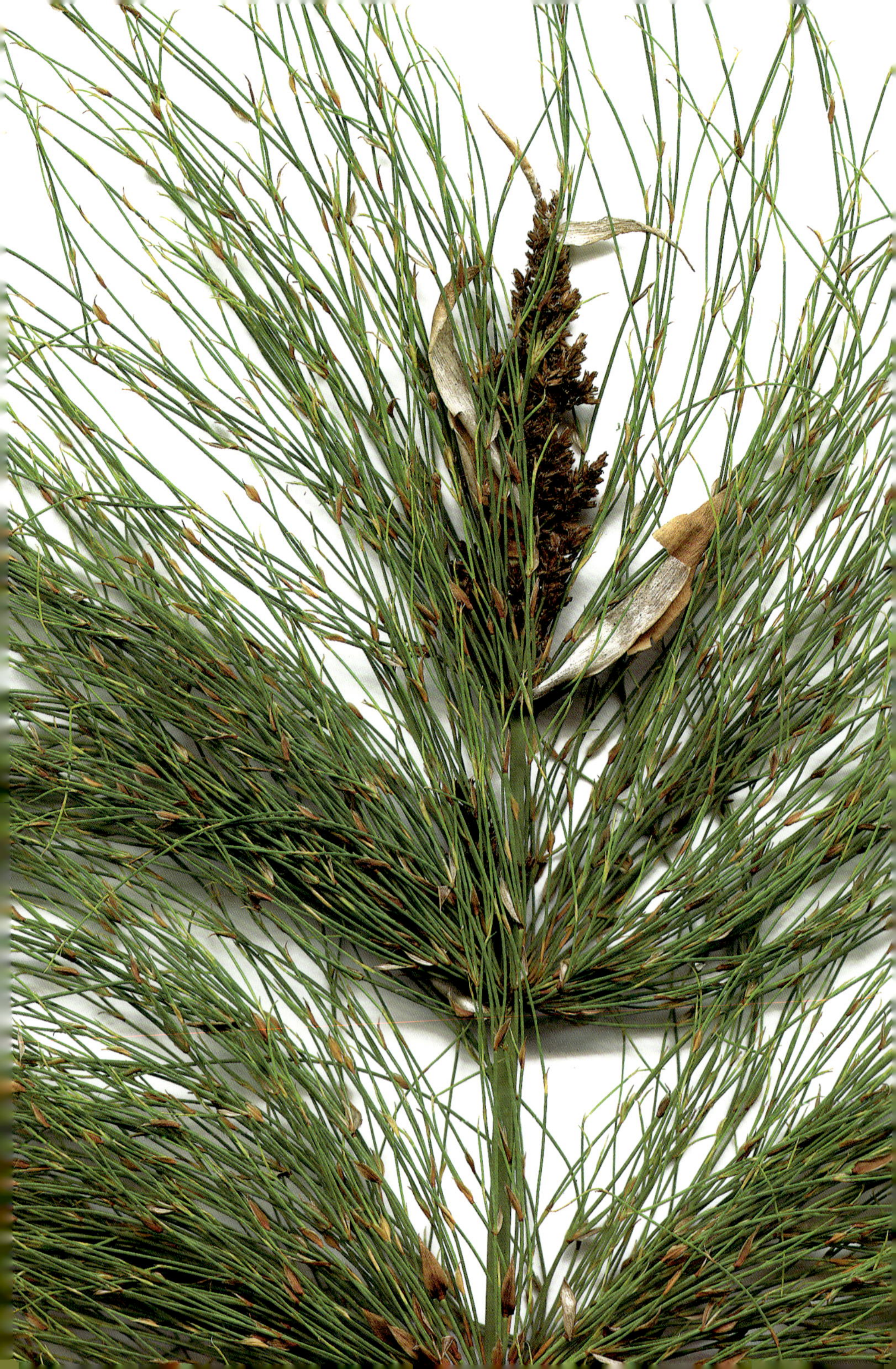

Elegia
E. capensis

This spectacular species is probably the most well known restio in cultivation. It decorates many spots in Kirstenbosch Garden and is also successfully grown in private gardens; it was originally described as an **Equisetum** *(horsetail), a worldwide one-genus member of the archaic flowerless family of the Equisetaceae*

Male and Female plants

INFLORESCENCES similar, at the tip of the main culm

CULMS branches clustered in whorls at the nodes along the culm

SHEATHS persistent

GROWTH FORM big plants, with strong rhizomes, reaching a height of about 3 m, forming big stands; plants resprout after fire

HABITAT mostly marshy areas, along streams and in seepages, in seasonally wet sandy soil derived from Table Mountain sandstone, from the coast to the interior

Elegia

	CULMS with branches clustered in whorls at the nodes along the culm SHEATHS persistent			INFLORESCENCE at the tip of the culm	
CULMS with branches not in whorls SHEATHS persistent	CULMS much branched	INFLORES-CENCE 3-5 cm long	OVARY with 2 slender styles, curled up in upper half, free parts of styles longer than the swollen base of the styles		
	CULMS much branched SHEATHS 10-15 mm long	INFLORES-CENCE 1.5-2.5 cm long	OVARY with 2 short, stout styles, free parts of the styles shorter than the swollen base of the styles	OVARY longer than the perianth	
	CULMS sparingly branched SHEATHS 3-6 cm long	INFLORES-CENCE 4-6 cm long		OVARY longer or as long as the perianth	

Elegia

17 Peninsula species, 35 species in total

E. capensis plants up to 3 m in height	HABITAT widespread, in marshy areas and along streams, often forming big uniform stands DISTRIBUTION from Clanwilliam to Uitenhage
E. stipularis	HABITAT well-drained sandy soils, near the coast and on foothills of mountains, below 200 m DISTRIBUTION from Malmesbury to Mossel Bay
E. prominens	HABITAT coastal flats, sand or peaty, marshy areas, at low altitudes DISTRIBUTION between Malmesbury and Bredasdorp
E. neesii	HABITAT moist and marshy areas DISTRIBUTION in the Northern Cederberg, between 1200-1500 m, and from Malmesbury and the Cape Peninsula to Humansdorp, from sea level to 1000 m

• *Species in shaded blocks are fully illustrated on pp. 56, 62*

Elegia

CULMS unbranched hollow	CULMS round in cross section		flowering the whole year round
CULMS unbranched, solid	CULMS flattened	BRACTS lacerated	SHEATHS sometimes persistent, on a slightly flattened culm
		BRACTS with smooth margins	SHEATHS at 45° angle to the culms, before dropping off
SHEATHS dropping off	CULMS round in cross section	CULMS up to 50 cm in height and at most 1.25 mm in diameter	CULMS tufted on the rhizome
			CULMS 10-20 cm in height, closely spaced on the rhizome
			CULMS 20-40 cm in height, distantly spaced on the rhizome
			CULMS up to 50 cm in height, tufted, on a short rhizome

Elegia

17 Peninsula species, 35 species in total

E. fistulosa	HABITAT sandy soils in marshy areas and along streams DISTRIBUTION widespread, from Malmesbury to Port Elizabeth
E. asperiflora plants with long rhizomes	HABITAT sandy soils in marshy areas and along streams, from sea level to 1500 m DISTRIBUTION widespread, from Clanwilliam to Port Alfred and from the Cape Peninsula to Laingsburg
E. coleura plants with long rhizomes	HABITAT sandy soils in seasonal marshes, from sea level to 1000 m DISTRIBUTION from Paarl to Humansdorp
E. verreauxii	HABITAT coastal forelands and shallow seasonal pans, mostly in sandy soils, below 150 m DISTRIBUTION between Malmesbury and Bredasdorp
E. squamosa	HABITAT hard, clayey soils, at the base of mountains, below 200 m DISTRIBUTION between Malmesbury and Bredasdorp
E. vaginulata	HABITAT sandy soils, marshy or peaty places, from sea level to 1500 m DISTRIBUTION from the Cederberg to Port Elizabeth
E. filacea	HABITAT general component in fynbos vegetation, in sandy soils, from sea level to 1800 m DISTRIBUTION widespread, from Clanwilliam to Port Elizabeth

• *Species in shaded blocks are fully illustrated on pp. 28, 54, 60*

Elegia

CULMS unbranched, solid, round in cross-section — at least 50 cm in height and 1.25 mm in diameter — SHEATHS dropping off	BRACTS with long awns	*awn*	INFLORESCENCE brushlike		
	BRACTS without awns, or at most with a short sharp point	INFLORESCENCE linear or tapering	SPATHES erect, overlapping and hiding the spikelets	FLOWERS < 5 mm, often less than 10 per node	
		INFLORESCENCE oblong	SPATHES somewhat overlapping, with spikelets often exposed	FLOWERS usually more than 10 per node	
				SPIKELETS with 5 to 8 flowers	
				SPIKELETS with 3 to 4 flowers	

Elegia

17 Peninsula species, 35 species in total

E. cuspidata SPATHES and sheaths chestnut-brown	HABITAT mostly marshy, and along streams, below 300 m DISTRIBUTION on the southern Cape Peninsula, in mountains between Kleinmond and Gordons Bay and in the sandveld near Mamre
E. racemosa SPATHES variegated, with margins much paler than the body, male ones often persistent, height variable	HABITAT steep rocky slopes in the mountains, between 600-1800 m DISTRIBUTION from Worcester to the Cape Peninsula and Uniondale
E. intermedia SPATHES papery, culms with scratchy surface	HABITAT seepages and swamps DISTRIBUTION endemic to Table Mountain
E. juncea SPATHES leathery, hiding the spikelets	HABITAT moist ground, from sea level to 1500 m DISTRIBUTION from Ceres to Uitenhage
E. fenestrata SPATHES leathery, partly hiding the spikelets, plants with long rhizomes	HABITAT coastal sand, seepages, or along streams DISTRIBUTION southern Cape Peninsula and on Bredasdorp coastal flats
E. thyrsifera SPATHES leathery, partly hiding the spikelets, plants tufted	HABITAT only sandstone-derived soils, in swamps and on riverbanks, between sea-level and 900 m DISTRIBUTION from the Cape Peninsula to Riversdale

• *Species in shaded blocks are fully illustrated on pp. 58, 60*

Askidiosperma
A. paniculatum

Male plant

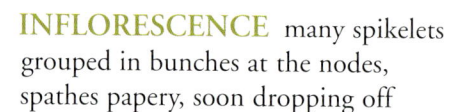

INFLORESCENCE many spikelets grouped in bunches at the nodes, spathes papery, soon dropping off

spikelets poorly defined, rather fluffy

bracts (and spathellae) transparent, longer than the flowers, becoming frayed and persisting as hairs on the older flowers

spikelet

Male and Female plants

CULMS unbranched

SHEATHS dropping off, leaving small, distinct, dark abscission rings at the nodes along the culms

GROWTH FORM plants tufted on a short rhizome, up to 80 cm in height

HABITAT and DISTRIBUTION absent from the Cape Peninsula, but widespread above 1000 m in the mountains of the Western Cape (except the Cederberg)

This genus contains 10 species in total

Askidiosperma

spikelet

Female plant

INFLORESCENCE several spikelets per culm, with papery spathes, overtopping the spikelets

spikelets with one or two flowers each

bracts (and spathellae) like those of the male, transparent and hairlike, longer than the flowers

FLOWERS round
- *perianth* tepals bony, deep brown to black, with rounded backs, petals as long as the sepals

- *styles* 3, feathery

- *fruit* a CAPSULE, 3-chambered

The transparent bracts easily distinguish this genus from the other two unbranched genera, **Chondropetalum** *and* **Elegia,** *all of which lose their sheaths*

Dovea
D. macrocarpa

Male plant

INFLORESCENCE many spikelets clustered in groups at several nodes of the inflorescence, with small spathes soon dropping off

spikelets small, paniculate, ripe anthers not protruding from the flowers, pollen released inside the tepals

bracts shorter than the flowers

Male and Female plants

CULMS branched and stout, 4-5 mm in diameter near the base of the plant

SHEATHS dropping off, leaving small, distinct, dark abscission rings at the nodes along the culms

GROWTH FORM plants spreading by well developed rhizomes, forming large patches or stands; up to 1 m in height

HABITAT and DISTRIBUTION this single species genus is absent from the Peninsula, but is common in dry fynbos between 100-1000 m on the Piketberg and the Olifants River mountains

Dovea

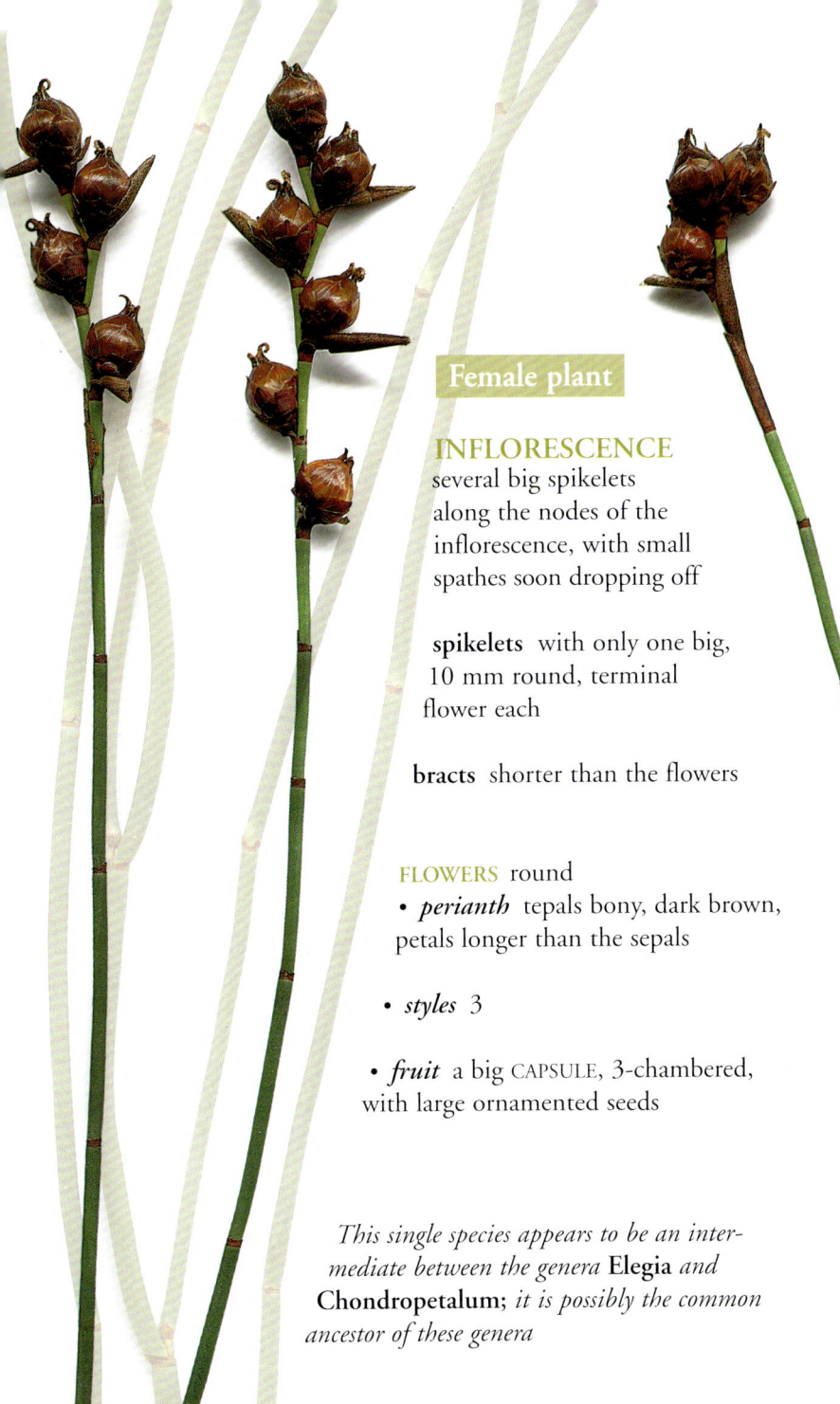

Female plant

INFLORESCENCE
several big spikelets along the nodes of the inflorescence, with small spathes soon dropping off

spikelets with only one big, 10 mm round, terminal flower each

bracts shorter than the flowers

FLOWERS round
• *perianth* tepals bony, dark brown, petals longer than the sepals

• *styles* 3

• *fruit* a big CAPSULE, 3-chambered, with large ornamented seeds

This single species appears to be an intermediate between the genera **Elegia** *and* **Chondropetalum**; *it is possibly the common ancestor of these genera*

Thamnochortus
T. lucens

Male plant

INFLORESCENCE many spikelets per culm, with small spathes

spikelets oblong, much longer than wide, pendulous, with many flowers; spikelets erect when young

bracts papery, longer than the flowers

Male and Female plants

CULMS unbranched, often with clusters of sterile shoots which appear at the nodes in the year after flowering

SHEATHS persistent, very long, tightly wrapped around the culm, the upper portion membranous, becoming frayed with age

GROWTH FORM plants tufted on a short rhizome, often with tangled clusters of sterile culms at the base and after flowering, at the nodes as well, up to 50 cm in height

HABITAT dry gravelly slopes, locally dominant or in small populations, from sea level to 800 m, very common in the Western Cape mountains

Thamnochortus

Female plant

INFLORESCENCE 1 to several spikelets per culm, with small spathes

spikelets stiffly erect, with many flowers

bracts cartilaginous, pointed, longer than the flowers

wing

flowers, x 5

frayed sheath

Gently rub the spikelets in your hands to release the delicate flowers

FLOWERS

• *perianth* tepals cartilaginous, lateral sepals winged, making the flower at least as wide as long (almost circular)

• *styles* 1, brushlike; *Thamnochortus* is the only genus with 1-styled flowers

• *fruit* a NUTLET, shed with the perianth attached; the winged sepals may be an adaptation to wind dispersal of the fruits

Thamnochortus
T. spicigerus

Male plant

INFLORESCENCE often more then 10 cm in length, with many spikelets and small spathes

spikelets spindle-shaped, pendulous, dark brown, with many flowers; spikelets erect when young

bracts papery, longer than the flowers

Male and Female plants

CULMS unbranched, stout, often with a slight curve

SHEATHS persistent, tightly wrapped around the culm, the upper halves membranous, becoming frayed with age

GROWTH FORM plants forming big stands by means of spreading rhizomes, up to 1.5 m in height

HABITAT sand on the coastal forelands

Thamnochortus

spikelet

Female plant

INFLORESCENCE in length similar to the male plant, with many spikelets and small spathes

spikelets stiffly erect, dark brown, egg-shaped and with many flowers

bracts cartilaginous, longer than the flowers

wing

flowers, x 5

To release the small flowers rub the spikelets gently in your hand

FLOWERS
- *perianth* tepals cartilaginous, with lateral sepals winged, making the flowers at least as wide as long (almost circular)

- *styles* 1, brushlike: this is a unique feature of the genus *Thamnochortus*

- *fruit* a NUTLET, shed with the perianth attached; the winged sepals probably aid in wind dispersal of the fruit

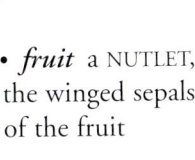

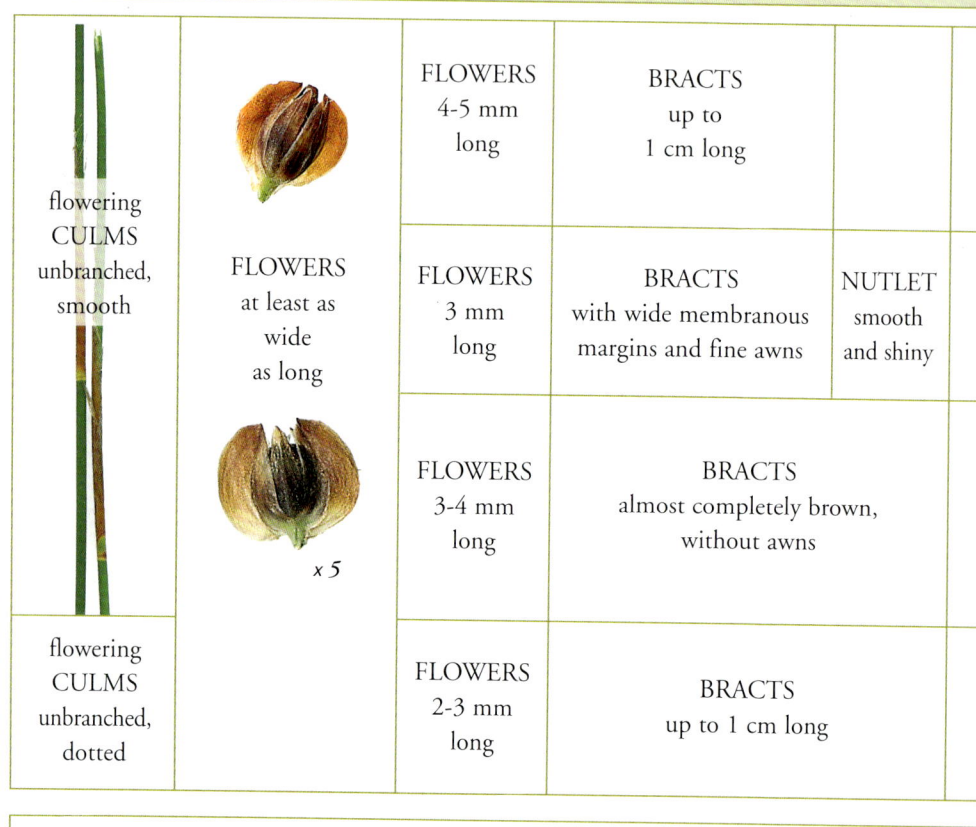

Thamnochortus

flowering CULMS unbranched, smooth	FLOWERS at least as wide as long *x 5*	FLOWERS 4-5 mm long	BRACTS up to 1 cm long	
		FLOWERS 3 mm long	BRACTS with wide membranous margins and fine awns	NUTLET smooth and shiny
		FLOWERS 3-4 mm long	BRACTS almost completely brown, without awns	
flowering CULMS unbranched, dotted		FLOWERS 2-3 mm long	BRACTS up to 1 cm long	

T. punctatus, *x 3.5*

T. sporadicus, *x 3.5*

Thamnochortus

13 Peninsula species, 34 species in total

PLANTS tufted	*T. lucens*	HABITAT dry gravelly slopes, from sea level to 800 m DISTRIBUTION from Saldanha and West Coast to the Cape Peninsula and from Tulbagh to Riviersonderend and Hermanus
CULMS evenly and closely spaced on a long rhizome	*T. arenarius*	HABITAT sandy soils, from sea level to 450 m DISTRIBUTION Cape Peninsula and along the coast from Cape Hangklip to Hermanus
	T. sporadicus	HABITAT sandy to stony soils, from sea level to 1000 m DISTRIBUTION from Piketberg and Ceres to the Cape Peninsula and the Riviersonderend Mountains
CULMS tufted on a rhizome	*T. punctatus*	HABITAT mostly dry coastal sandy flats DISTRIBUTION from Nieuwoudtville to the Cape Peninsula

flowers

T. lucens, *x 3.5*

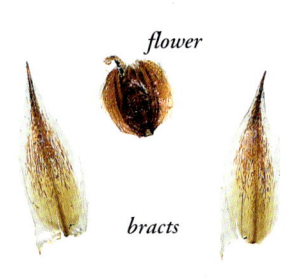

flower

bracts

T. arenarius, *x 3.5*

• Species in shaded block is fully illustrated on p. 74

79

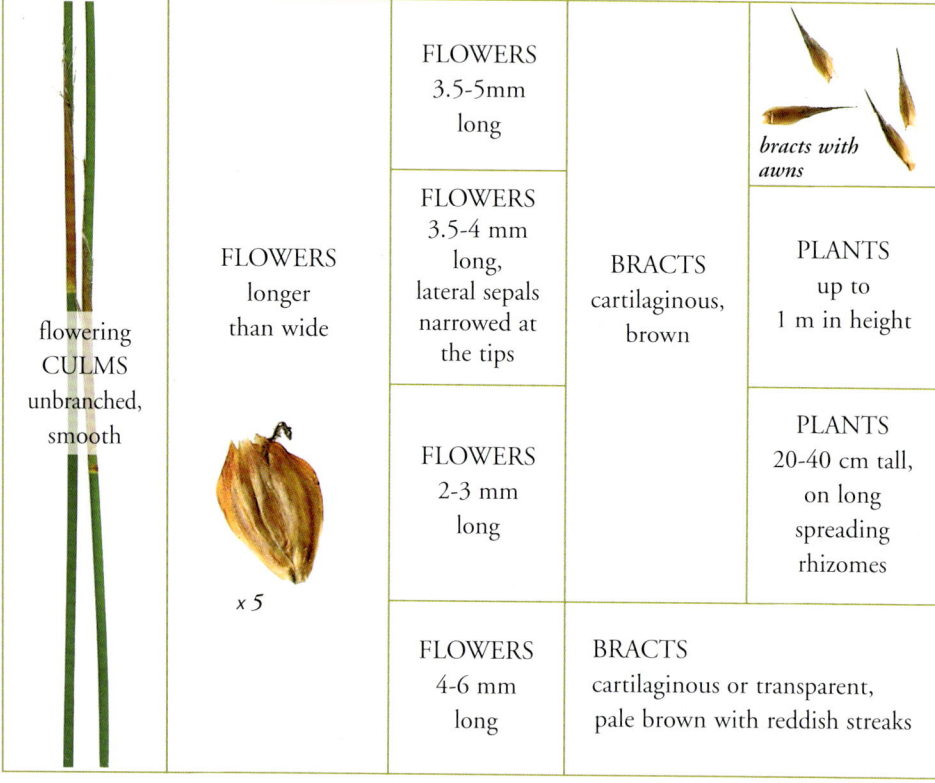

Thamnochortus

flowering CULMS unbranched, smooth	FLOWERS longer than wide x 5	FLOWERS 3.5-5mm long	BRACTS cartilaginous, brown	*bracts with awns*
		FLOWERS 3.5-4 mm long, lateral sepals narrowed at the tips		PLANTS up to 1 m in height
		FLOWERS 2-3 mm long		PLANTS 20-40 cm tall, on long spreading rhizomes
		FLOWERS 4-6 mm long	BRACTS cartilaginous or transparent, pale brown with reddish streaks	

flowers

bracts

T. obtusus, x 3.5

flower

bract

T. guthrieae, x 3.5

Thamnochortus

13 Peninsula species, 34 species in total

 *flowers*	*T. nutans*	HABITAT south-east cloud belt, above 600 m DISTRIBUTION endemic to Table Mountain and Constantiaberg
exposed strips between the sepal bases	*T. fraternus*	HABITAT limestone and coastal dunes DISTRIBUTION around the coast of False Bay, Bredasdorp
one or no exposed strips between the sepal bases	*T. obtusus*	HABITAT dry sand, below 300 m DISTRIBUTION along the coastal forelands from Malmesbury to Bredasdorp
	T. guthrieae	HABITAT hard gravelly to sandy soils, from sea level to 600 m DISTRIBUTION from Malmesbury to Bredasdorp

flowers

bracts

T. nutans, *x 3.5*

Thamnochortus

flowering CULMS unbranched

CULMS smooth

CULMS velvety to hairy

INFLORESCENCE more than 10 cm long

FLOWERS at least as wide as long, hidden by the bracts

FLOWERS wider than long

lateral sepal wings more than 2 mm wide and protruding from the sides of the bracts

wing of flower

bract

x 3.5

flowers

T. insignis, x 3.5

Thamnochortus

13 Peninsula species, 34 species in total

SPIKELETS medium brown	*T. insignis*	HABITAT limestone hills or sandy flats DISTRIBUTION coastal forelands from Bredasdorp to Riversdale. As a result of being used as thatching reed and seed being spread in transport of the thatch, now also growing at Klaasjagersbos and some other places on the Peninsula
SPIKELETS light brown	*T. erectus*	HABITAT hills and flats of coastal forelands, mostly in sand DISTRIBUTION from Darling to Knysna
SPIKELETS dark brown	*T. spicigerus*	HABITAT sand DISTRIBUTION on the Cape Flats, Hopefield and the sandveld from Langebaan to Somerset West
PLANTS with well-developed rhizomes	*T. fruticosus*	HABITAT below 600 m DISTRIBUTION between Ceres, the Cape Peninsula and Caledon

flowers

bract

T. spicigerus, x 3.5

spikelet

wing of flower

bract

flower

T. fruticosus, x 3.5

• Species in shaded block is fully illustrated on p. 76

Thamnochortus

BRANCHES fertile	FLOWERS wider than long	FLOWERS 2-3 mm long	
	FLOWERS longer than wide	FLOWERS 2-3 mm long	
BRANCHES usually sterile	FLOWERS longer than wide	FLOWERS 2-3 mm long	
		FLOWERS 4-6 mm long	
BRANCHES sterile	FLOWERS wider than long	FLOWERS 3-4 mm long	
		FLOWERS 3 mm long	

flowering CULMS with branches

flowers

bracts

T. gracilis, x 3.5

Thamnochortus

13 Peninsula species, 34 species in total

	T. gracilis	HABITAT amongst rocks or in sandy places on dry mountain slopes and plateaus DISTRIBUTION from the Cape Peninsula to Franschhoek, Genadendal and Hermanus
	T. levynsiae	HABITAT steep rocky slopes or ledges, from 450-900 m DISTRIBUTION confined to the Cape Peninsula
	T. obtusus	HABITAT dry sandy places of coastal forelands, below 300 m DISTRIBUTION from Malmesbury to Bredasdorp
SHEATHS on sterile branches without awns	*T. guthrieae*	HABITAT hard gravelly to sandy soil, from sea level to 450 m DISTRIBUTION from Malmesbury to Bredasdorp
BRACTS almost completely brown, without awns	*T. sporadicus* culms evenly spaced on a long rhizome	HABITAT sandy to stony soils, from sea level to 1000 m DISTRIBUTION from Piketberg and Ceres to the Cape Peninsula and the Riviersonderend Mountains
BRACTS with wide membranous margins, finely awned	*T. arenarius* culms evenly spaced on a long rhizome; nutlet smooth, shiny, easily separated from the perianth	HABITAT sandy places, from sea level to 450 m DISTRIBUTION on the Cape Peninsula and along the coast from Cape Hangklip to Hermanus

flowers

T. levynsiae, x 3.5

Staberoha
S. banksii

Male plant

INFLORESCENCE 1-10 spikelets per culm, each with a small spathe

spikelets bell-shaped, pendulous, clustered at several nodes, and with many flowers

bracts cartilaginous, spreading almost at right angles to the axis of the spikelet, totally hiding the flowers

Male and Female plants

CULMS unbranched

SHEATHS persistent, tightly wrapped around the culm

GROWTH FORM plants tufted on a very short rhizome, up to about 60 cm in height; this is the tallest of all *Staberoha* species, with the largest spikelets

HABITAT sand between rocks, from 100-1000 m, but mostly at lower altitudes, in the southern Peninsula

Staberoha

Female plant

INFLORESCENCE 1-6 spikelets per culm, each with a small spathe

spikelets stiffly erect, cylindrical, with many flowers

bracts 6-10 mm long, much longer than and completely hiding the flowers, more than 10 per spikelet

FLOWERS

- *perianth* tepals 1.5-2.5 mm long, papery, lateral sepals keeled

- *styles* 3, feathery, flat

- *fruit* a NUTLET

Staberoha

BRACTS < 1 cm long	FLOWERS with lateral sepals keeled	FLOWERS similar, but much smaller than *S. banksii*, < 3 mm	***S. vaginata*** plants tufted, very similar to but smaller than *S. banksii;*
BRACTS > 1 cm long		FLOWERS, x 3.5 — styles — keel > 3 mm	***S. banksii*** plants tufted
In all species the small flowers are hidden deep down within the hard bracts Carefully bend back the bracts and you will find them Even on old spikelets there are always some flowers left	FLOWERS with lateral sepals winged	FLOWERS, x 3.5 *petals pointed* — wings frilly	***S. distachyos*** plants spreading on a rhizome
		FLOWERS, x 3.5 *petals rounded* — wings lacerated	***S. cernua*** plants tufted

Staberoha

4 Peninsula species, 9 species in total

HABITAT rocky areas, from 450-1200 m
DISTRIBUTION from the Cederberg to the Kogelberg, confined to Echo Valley on the Cape Peninsula

HABITAT sand between rocks, from sea level to 1600 m
DISTRIBUTION from the Hex River Mountains to Bredasdorp

HABITAT widespread on clayey, sandy or gravelly soils, from sea level to 1000 m
DISTRIBUTION from Van Rhynsdorp to Bredasdorp

HABITAT widespread on rocky soils, from sea level to 1000 m
DISTRIBUTION from Ceres and Piketberg to the Cape Peninsula and the Swartberg and Kouga mountains

• Species in shaded block is fully illustrated on p. 86

♀

♂

Young Staberoha *plants display spectacular deep red - copper coloured inflorescences*

Rhodocoma
R. fruticosa

Male plant

INFLORESCENCE numerous branchlets with many spikelets clustered at a few nodes; spathes small, becoming frayed with age

spikelets spindle-shaped, pendulous with many flowers each; spikelets erect when young

bracts papery

Male and Female plants

CULMS unbranched, blue-green, occasionally with clusters of sterile branches at the nodes of the older culms

SHEATHS persistent, very long, closely wrapped around the culm, with upper halves membranous becoming frayed with age

GROWTH FORM plants spreading on a rhizome, forming small patches, up to 1 m in height

Rhodocoma

flowers

Female plant

INFLORESCENCE many spikelets per culm; spathes small, becoming frayed with age

spikelets clustered at the nodes of the inflorescence

bracts papery, shorter than the flowers

FLOWERS
- *perianth* cartilaginous, petals as long as the sepals

- *styles* 3, feathery

- *fruit* a CAPSULE, 3-chambered

HABITAT and DISTRIBUTION widespread up to the Natal Drakensberg, on sandstone and lateritic soils; this species used to occur on the Cape Peninsula on the flats of Claremont, but is now extinct there

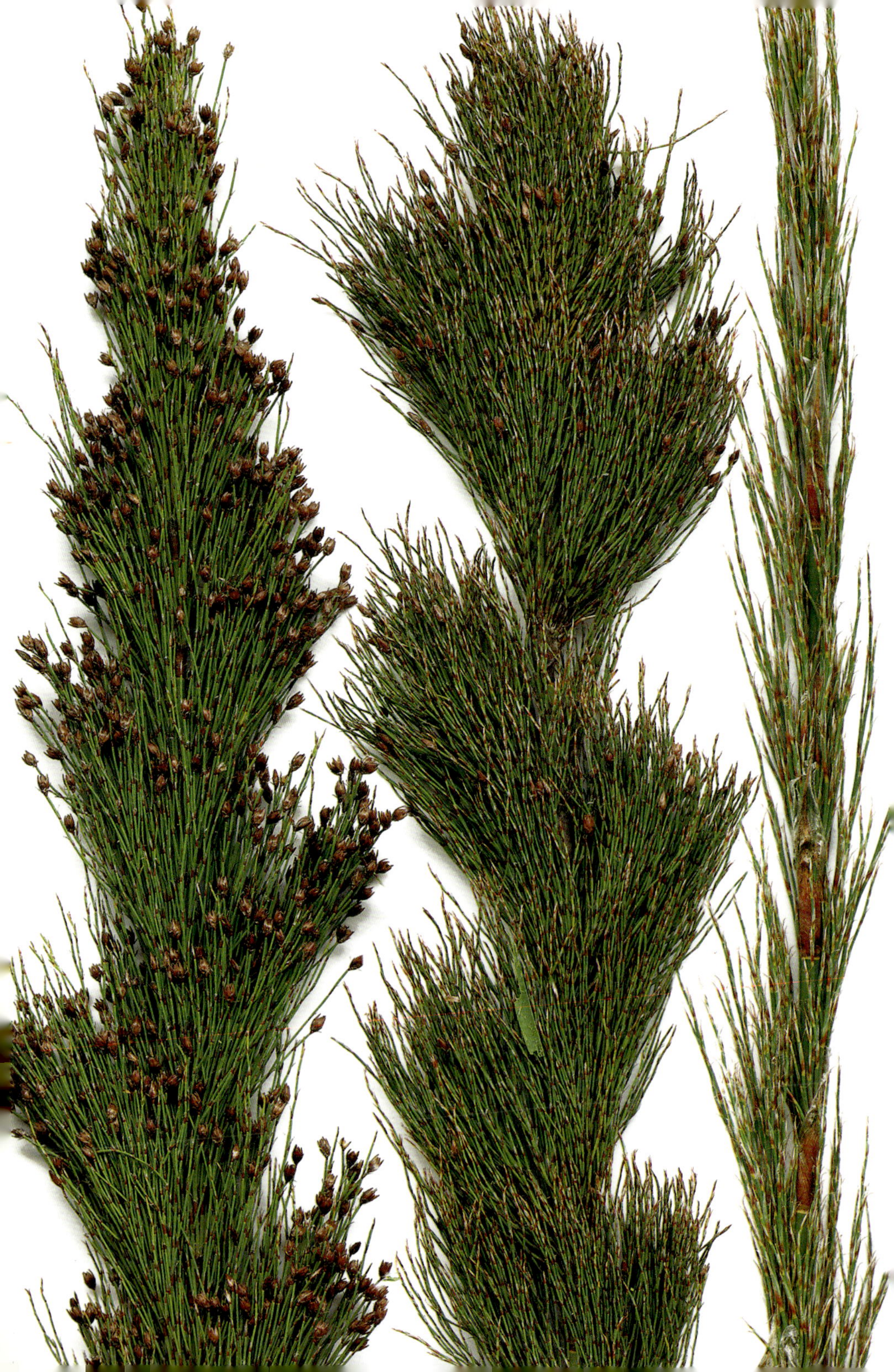

Rhodocoma
R. capensis

Male and Female plants

INFLORESCENCE one small spikelet at the tip of each branch; male and female spikelets very similar (except for the flowers)

FEMALE FLOWERS
- *styles* 3, deep pink
- *fruit* a CAPSULE, 3-chambered

CULMS many short branches in whorls at the nodes along the main culm

GROWTH FORM plants bushy, up to 1.5 m in height, growing in big clumps; this species is very atypical of the genus *Rhodocoma*

HABITAT sandstone and quartzite soils, often forming big stands in loamy soils along valley bottoms

DISTRIBUTION absent from the Cape Peninsula, growing along the arid inland margins of the Cape Fold mountains

This genus contains 8 species in total

spikelet

Hypodiscus
H. aristatus

Male plant

INFLORESCENCE 1 to several spikelets per culm with spathes curved backwards

spikelets compact, spiky, spindle-shaped, with many flowers, varying in size from 10-20 mm

bracts bony, very spiky and pointed, longer than the flowers

older male spikelets

Male and Female plants

CULMS unbranched

SHEATHS persistent, tightly wrapped around the culm

bracts

GROWTH FORM plants tufted on a well developed rhizome, forming distinctive dark coloured tussocks, scattered in the vegetation, up to 0.5 m in height, resprouting after fire

HABITAT widespread in well drained sandy soil, often on rocky mountain sides, from sea level to 1500 m

Hypodiscus

styles

spathe

Female plant

INFLORESCENCE 1 to several spikelets per culm with spathes curved backwards

spikelets compact, spiky, spindle-shaped, bigger than the males, with only 1 terminal flower each; they enlarge dramatically from flowering until the fruit is ripe

bracts bony, very spiky, and pointed, longer than the flowers

FLOWERS
• *perianth* tepals membranous, petals as long as the sepals

• *styles* 2, long and fluffy, joined at the base, projecting from the top of the spikelet

• *fruit* a NUT, smooth and shiny, dark brown to black, hard and woody, 8 mm long, round in cross section, and with a pale green elaiosome (see species key)

older female spikelet

nuts with elaiosomes

Hypodiscus
H. willdenowia

Male plant

INFLORESCENCE 1 spikelet at the tip of each culm, with a small spathe

spikelets spindle-shaped, with several flowers

bracts several, longer than the flowers

Male and Female plants

CULMS unbranched, striped, flattened

SHEATHS persistent, closely wrapped around the culm, green, upper margins membranous

GROWTH FORM fairly insignificant looking plants, spreading by means of long rhizomes, with culms often forming long straight lines, or growing as spreading patches; up to about 20 cm in height

HABITAT sandy soils, often seasonally wet, from sea level to 1200 m

Hypodiscus

Female plant

INFLORESCENCE 1 spikelet at the tip of each culm, with a small spathe

spikelets small, spindle-shaped, with only 1 terminal flower each

bracts several per spikelet

FLOWERS
• *perianth* tepals membranous, longer than the nutlet, petals as long as the sepals

• *styles* 2, long and fluffy, joined at the base

• *fruit* a NUT with elaiosome, overtopped by the perianth

nut

Hypodiscus

CULMS striped	CULMS flattened	NUT, x 3.5 — *elaiosome*	**H. willdenowia** plants with long rhizomes	
	CULMS round in cross section	NUT, x 3.5 — *elaiosome (dried out)*	**H. argenteus** flowers without a perianth	*bracts silvery* x 0.5
CULMS smooth		NUT, x 3.5 — *irregularly lobed*	**H. rugosus**	
		nut cap smooth — NUT, x 3.5 — *tepal* — *elaiosome*	**H. aristatus**	
		nut cap with 1-3 rows of small teeth — NUT, x 3.5 — *elaiosome*	**H. albo-aristatus** culms with only one sheath at the base or in the middle	

Hypodiscus

5 Peninsula species, 15 species in total

HABITAT sandy, seasonally wet areas, from sea level to 1200 m
DISTRIBUTION from Ceres to Grahamstown; in southern Cape on coastal plateaux; in western Cape up to 1200 m

HABITAT dry, well drained stony slopes, 100 m-1200 m
DISTRIBUTION from the North Cederberg to the Cape Peninsula and Riversdale

HABITAT sandy or clayey soils in seasonally wet areas, flats and hills of coastal forelands below 450 m
DISTRIBUTION between Malmesbury and Riversdale

HABITAT widespread on well drained sandy soils, from sea level to 1500 m
DISTRIBUTION ubiquitous in the Cape, from the Cederberg to Humansdorp

HABITAT well drained wet or dry mountain slopes, from 100-1600 m, often on shale
DISTRIBUTION from Tulbagh to Cape Peninsula on to Oudtshoorn and Humansdorp

*H.albo-aristatus
with 2 nuts*

• *Species in shaded blocks are fully illustrated on pp. 94, 96*

Nevillea
N. obtusissima

Male plant

INFLORESCENCE 2 or 3 spikelets at the tip of the culm, with small spathes

spikelets oblong, cone-like, dark brown, compact, and with many flowers

bracts bony, round, tightly overlapping, upper margins darker than the body

Male and Female plants

CULMS unbranched, dull green

SHEATHS persistent, closely wrapped around the culm and with long stiff awns

GROWTH FORM plants with short rhizomes, forming large clumps often more than 1 m in diameter, up to about 70 cm in height, resprouting after fire

HABITAT usually in marshy areas in the mountains

DISTRIBUTION this species is absent from the Cape Peninsula. It grows on the mountains between Elgin and Kleinmond, between 300-1000 m. There is only one other species in this genus, *N. singularis,* which is endemic to Kanonkop at Genadendal

Nevillea

spathe

Female plant

INFLORESCENCE several spikelets per culm, hidden by tightly overlapping spathes; this inflorescence is very different from that of the male, the most extreme example of sexual dimorphism amongst the restios

spikelets with several flowers each

bracts bony, tightly overlapping around each other

FLOWERS

• *perianth* membranous, lateral sepals keeled

• *styles* 2, maroon, long and curly, fused at the base

• *fruit* a NUTLET, 2-chambered, with 1 or 2 seeds (unusual feature)

spathe removed to expose spikelet with two flowers, of which only the styles are visible, x 2.5

Ceratocaryum
C. argenteum

Male plant

INFLORESCENCE big and bushy, white to silvery; no distinct spikelets but flowers grouped into many panicles at the nodes, with large spathes soon dropping off

bracts and **tepals** equal, linear, papery and white

Male and Female plants

CULMS unbranched, stout, in parts slightly hollow

SHEATHS persistent, tightly wrapped around the culm; upper margins membranous and finely lacerated

GROWTH FORM plants growing on a spreading rhizome, forming big tussocks, up to 2 m in height

HABITAT on sandy soils below 300 m

DISTRIBUTION absent from the Cape Peninsula, but widespread on the Bredasdorp and Riversdale plains

This genus contains 6 species in total

male flowers, x 5

Ceratocaryum

Female plant

INFLORESCENCE
several big spikelets clustered at the nodes, partially hidden by the big spathes

spikelets with 1 flower each

bracts papery, overtopping the single flower

FLOWERS
- *perianth* tepals small, transparent, all equally long, much shorter than the nut

- *styles* 2, stout

- *fruit* a NUT, ca.10 mm in diameter, almost round, pitted, woody, and without an elaiosome

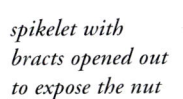

spikelet with bracts opened out to expose the nut

spathe

Willdenowia
W. glomerata

Male plant

INFLORESCENCE flowers not grouped into spikelets, but stalked and forming a large confused panicle, partially enclosed by a large spathe

bracts and **tepals** of the flowers transparent and linear

Male and Female plants

CULMS branched

SHEATHS persistent, loosely wrapped around the culm, the upper third membranous and decaying on the older culms

GROWTH FORM plants tufted, on a short rhizome, up to 80 cm in height, the older bigger bushes often looking very untidy

HABITAT widespread on dry stony mountain slopes, from 500-1500 m

sheath, x 2

Willdenowia

bracts

nut

Female plant

INFLORESCENCE
1 spikelet at the tip of each culm

spikelets with only 1 terminal flower each

bracts several, overtopping the nut

FLOWERS
- *perianth* tepals small, membranous, not touching at the margins (see species key)

- *styles* 2, free to the base, mostly hidden by the bracts

- *fruit* a NUT, dark brown to black, hard, woody, pitted, round in cross section, 5-9 mm long and with an elaiosome

Flowering spikelet with some bracts removed to expose the styles, x 1.5

Willdenowia

	CULMS striped × 3.5	NUT without elaiosome	× 3.5 — tepals
		NUT with elaiosome	× 3.5 — tepals — elaiosome
CULMS branched	CULMS smooth × 3.5	NUT with elaiosome	× 3.5 tepals not touching at the base, or absent — elaiosome
			× 3.5 tepals wider towards the base and overlapping — elaiosome
		NUT without elaiosome	
CULMS unbranched, slender		NUT without elaiosome	× 3.5 — scalloped surface — tepals

6 Peninsula species, 11 species in total

W. incurvata	HABITAT coastal sand DISTRIBUTION widespread, from Namaqualand to False Bay, local in intermontane valleys
W. sulcata	HABITAT sandy or rocky well-drained soils, from sea level to 1800 m DISTRIBUTION in Western Cape from the Cederberg to Caledon and the Cape Peninsula
W. glomerata	HABITAT dry stony slopes, from 50-1500 m DISTRIBUTION almost ubiquitous in mountains of the Cederberg to Port Elizabeth, but rare in the southern Cape
W. teres	HABITAT mountains and coastal sandy soils, from sea level to 1500 m DISTRIBUTION widespread in the Cape, from the Kamiesberg to Uitenhage
W. affinis	HABITAT only known from the original collection from the northern slopes of Table Mountain
W. humilis	HABITAT moist sand, from sea level to about 1200 m DISTRIBUTION from the Cederberg to the Caledon coast

• *Species in shaded block is fully illustrated on p. 104*

Mastersiella
M. digitata

Male plant

INFLORESCENCE several spikelets per culm with a small spathe each

spikelets conelike, straw-coloured, with many flowers each

bracts cartilaginous

Male and Female plants

CULMS branched

SHEATHS persistent, tightly wrapped around the culm

GROWTH FORM plants tufted but rather floppy, in clumps up to 30 cm in height, all culms rising from a single central point

HABITAT dry sandy or rocky slopes, below 400 m, often locally common; plants killed by fire

DISTRIBUTION between the Cape Peninsula, Villiersdorp and the Potberg (near Bredasdorp); this is the only species found on the Peninsula out of a total of 3 species

Mastersiella

nutlets

Female plant

INFLORESCENCE
1 slender spikelet at the tip of each culm, with a small spathe each

spikelets compact, with only 1 flower each

bracts bony, tightly wrapped around the single flower

FLOWERS
• *perianth* tepals membranous

• *styles* 2, feathery, free to the base

• *fruit* a NUTLET, shiny, black, overtopped by the perianth and with a minute elaiosome

spikelet, x 5

nutlets, x 5

109

Anthochortus
A. crinalis

Known amongst hikers as 'orgy grass', this small restio resembles big, soft luscious cushions. The illustrations are of handfuls of culms pulled out of these soft hummocks

Male and Female plants

CULMS finely branched and with warts

SHEATHS persistent, closely wrapped around the culm, speckled and with long hairlike awns (see pp. 112, 113)

GROWTH FORM older plants densely packed, with tangled culms, forming big soft round cushions (see photo on p. 112); these can grow into thick mats covering substantial areas

HABITAT high altitude marshy places, in shallow soil over rock and on damp rock ledges, from 600-1800 m

Anthochortus

FEMALE INFLORESCENCE
1 spikelet (with 1 flower) at the tip of each culm, bracts and spathes like those of the male plant

FLOWERS
- *styles* 2
- *fruit* a NUTLET, soft-walled, ca. 4 mm long

Anthochortus

	CULMS lightly ridged to 4-angled	SPIKELETS solitary, stalked, and lateral	BRACTS papery, longer than the flower
CULMS branched SHEATHS persistent	CULMS smooth to warty	SPIKELETS one (♀) to several (♂) at the tip of the culms; spathes with hairlike awns	BRACTS papery, with straight tips
		SPIKELETS one (♀) to several (♂) at the tip of the culms	BRACTS cartilaginous with membranous margins, speckled and with long, pointed, recurved tips

Anthochortus crinalis *on Table Mountain near Maclear's Beacon (see also p. 5)*

A. crinalis,
x 3.5

Anthochortus

3 Peninsula species, 6 species in total

A. capensis	HABITAT marshes and marshy stream banks, up to 300 m DISTRIBUTION endemic to Muizenberg Mountain and the Cape of Good Hope Nature Reserve	
A. laxiflorus	HABITAT high altitude marshy areas DISTRIBUTION the Cape Peninsula and Hottentots Holland Mountains	
A. crinalis	HABITAT marshy places, shallow soil over rock, and damp rock ledges in mountains, from 600-1800 m DISTRIBUTION in the mountains from Bainskloof to the Cape Peninsula and Riversdale	*A. capensis*

• *Species in shaded block is fully illustrated on p. 110*

spikelet

♂

sheath

♀

A. crinalis,
x 3.5

♀

nut

A. capensis,
x 3.5

Hydrophilus
H. rattrayi

Male plant

INFLORESCENCE similar to the female inflorescence except for the somewhat smaller flowers

bracts

Male and Female plants

CULMS sparsely branched

SHEATHS tightly wrapped around the culms

GROWTH FORM plants forming clumps, spreading by rhizomes, often tangled with other plants

HABITAT on streambanks and in wet seeps in sandstone or quartzite mountains, from 900-1500 m

DISTRIBUTION this single-species genus is absent from the Cape Peninsula, but widespread along the inland margins of the Cape Fold Mountains

Hydrophilus

flowers

Female plant

INFLORESCENCE several spikelets per culm, with small, papery spathes

spikelets with many flowers

bracts papery, silvery white, with a red brown streak in the centre, pointed and closely overlapping

FLOWERS

- *perianth* inner tepals membranous, lateral sepals keeled

- *styles* 2, lightly fused at the base

- *fruit* a NUTLET, ca.3 mm long

spikelet

Cannomois
C. virgata

Male plant

INFLORESCENCE this illustration shows only part of a spectacular young male inflorescence; this one was almost 50 cm long, with hundreds of small spindle-shaped to spherical spikelets on branchlets, clustered at the nodes

Male and Female plants

CULMS very stout, branched

SHEATHS persistent, closely wrapped around the culm

GROWTH FORM plants varying from short and spreading to large, bamboo-like, and tufted, up to 3 m in height, growing on a strong rhizome

HABITAT common along streams or wet mountain slopes, from sea level to 1800 m

DISTRIBUTION widespread in the mountains of the Cape from Nieuwoudtville to Uitenhage; out of a total of 8 species this is the only one found on the Peninsula

Cannomois
C. virgata

Female plant

INFLORESCENCE 1 spikelet at the tip of each culm, with small spathes

spikelets rather fat, spindle-shaped, with several flowers each

bracts bony, tightly overlapping, difficult to separate

FLOWERS
• *perianth* tepals membranous, almost as long as the nut

• *styles* 2, free to the base, long and feathery

• *fruit* a NUT, black, ca.9 mm long, flattened on one side, smooth and woody, with a very small white elaiosome; this is the only genus that has several big nuts in each single spikelet

lower part of young shoot

tip of young shoot

Cannomois

spikelet

nuts

Cannomois
C. parviflora

Male plant

INFLORESCENCE numerous spikelets per culm, with spathes overtopping the spikelets but soon dropping off

spikelets elliptical, with many flowers

bracts cartilaginous, longer than the flowers

Male and Female plants

CULMS unbranched

SHEATHS persistent, tightly wrapped around the culm

GROWTH FORM plants forming big clumps, up to 60 cm in height, spreading by means of creeping rhizomes

HABITAT mostly dry sandy soils, on the coastal forelands or in the mountains, between 100-1300 m; this species varies geographically; the illustrated plant comes from the sandveld at Hopefield

DISTRIBUTION absent from the Cape Peninsula but common and widespread from Nieuwoudtville to Swellendam and Houw Hoek

Cannomois

Female plant

INFLORESCENCE 1-2 spikelets per culm, partially hidden by the spathes

spikelets with several flowers

bracts bony, tightly curved into spindle-shaped spikelets

FLOWERS
- *perianth* tepals transparent, small, unequal in length

- *styles* 2, free to the base, brushlike

- *fruit* a NUT, shiny, black, ca.8 mm long, flattened on one side and with a white elaiosome

— *spikelet*

x 3.5

Calopsis
C. paniculata

Male and Female plants

CULMS sparsely branched, stout

SHEATHS persistent, the upper portion pale membranous and soon decaying

GROWTH FORM plants tufted on strong rhizomes, forming big tussocks or occupying extensive areas, up to 3 m in height; the lower parts of the culms bamboo-like; taller, but in appearance much like *Restio tetragonus* (p. 149)

Calopsis

MALE and FEMALE INFLORESCENCE a big, much-branched panicle, 15-20 cm long, with hundreds of spikelets

FEMALE FLOWERS
- *perianth* tepals papery, lateral sepals keeled

- *styles* 3, feathery

- *fruit* a NUTLET

HABITAT a very typical element of streamside vegetation, sometimes in marshy areas, on sandstone or quartzite soils, mostly below 600 m

Calopsis
C. viminea

Male plant

INFLORESCENCE 1 to several spikelets per branch, with small spathes

spikelets with several flowers

bracts cartilaginous, round-backed, longer than the flowers

Male and Female plants

CULMS sparsely branched

SHEATHS persistent, more or less flat and loosely wrapped around the culm, the tip extended into an awn

GROWTH FORM untidy looking plants, rather tangled and straggly, growing on a very short rhizome

HABITAT all kinds of soils, from sea level to 1500 m

Calopsis

Female plant

INFLORESCENCE

several spikelets per culm, with small spathes

spikelets slender, spindle-shaped with several flowers

bracts cartilaginous, longer than the flowers

FLOWERS

- *perianth* tepals papery, lateral sepals keeled and hairy

- *styles* 3, feathery, often red

- *fruit* a NUTLET

Except for the tall handsome **Calopsis paniculata** *(p. 122)* all other species of this genus, including this one, are rather small and form untidy clumps

Calopsis

SHEATHS with upper part membranous and deciduous x 5	INFLORESCENCE a much branched panicle, 15-20 cm long	BRACTS overlapping lateral SEPALS not keeled
	INFLORESCENCE less than 10 cm long	lateral SEPALS pointed, smooth, somewhat keeled
SHEATHS without membranous margins x 3.5	SHEATHS wrapped around the culm, and with long awns	SPIKELETS small, 2-4 mm, 1 per culm
	SHEATHS almost flat, often spreading x 3.5	lateral SEPALS hairy
		lateral SEPALS hairless SHEATHS with awns

Calopsis

5 Peninsula species, 23 species in total

C. paniculata big bamboo-like plant	HABITAT along streams and sometimes marshy places, on sandstone or quartzite soils, mostly below 600 m DISTRIBUTION from the Cederberg to Natal, south of Durban
C. membranacea	HABITAT often on steep mountain slopes, in dense vegetation, from 100-1000 m DISTRIBUTION from Tulbagh to the Cape Peninsula and Hermanus and along the Riviersonderend mountains and Langeberg to George
C. gracilis	HABITAT often on stabilized sand but also on stony mountain slopes, from sea level to 450 m DISTRIBUTION endemic to the southern Cape Peninsula
C. viminea	HABITAT all kinds of soils, from sea level to 1500 m DISTRIBUTION from the Kamiesberg to Laingsburg, the Cape Peninsula and Bredasdorp
C. fruticosa	HABITAT limestones, coastal sands, sandstone and clay, along the coast DISTRIBUTION from the Cape Peninsula to the mouth of the Duiwenhoks River (near Riversdale)

young culm of C. paniculata

x 3.5

• *Species in shaded blocks are fully illustrated on pp. 122, 124*

Ischyrolepis
I. capensis

A rather straggly, unobtrusive plant, but so common on dry soils that it deserves its place in this book

Male plant

INFLORESCENCE 1-2 spikelets per culm, with small spathes

spikelets compact, spindle-shaped, with 2 to many flowers

bracts with distinctive, recurved awns

Male and Female plants

CULMS branched, with warts, often with sterile growths at the nodes of the older culms

SHEATHS persistent, flat or loosely wrapped around the culms

GROWTH FORM plants tufted, often rather prostrate, frequently with mats of sterile growth at the base

HABITAT widespread, common on sandy, gravelly and even shaly soils, at all altitudes, often in slightly disturbed areas

Ischyrolepis

Female plant

INFLORESCENCE similar to that of the male, except for the slightly bigger spikelets

FLOWERS
- *perianth* tepals bony, lateral sepals keeled
- *styles* 2, joined at the base
- *fruit* a CAPSULE, 2-chambered

On the older flowers, when the free parts of the 2 styles have withered away, the joined bases remain on the fruit (ovary and capsule) as a persistent small woody peg, the **stylopodium**

This is diagnostic of all species of the genus *Ischyrolepis* and a particular feature that distinguishes this genus from the genus *Restio*, to which it is very similar in many other aspects

ovary, x 5

Ischyrolepis
I. cincinnata

Male plant

INFLORESCENCE 1 to 2 spikelets at the tip of each culm

spikelets small, compact, with several flowers each

Ischyrolepis

Female plant

INFLORESCENCE similar to the male except for the slightly bigger, single-flowered spikelets

FLOWERS
• *perianth* lateral sepals keeled and hairy, becoming woody with age

• *styles* 2, purple, joined at the base, remaining as a small woody peg (stylopodium) on the fruit of older flower (see also pp. 129, 136)

• *fruit* a CAPSULE, 2-chambered

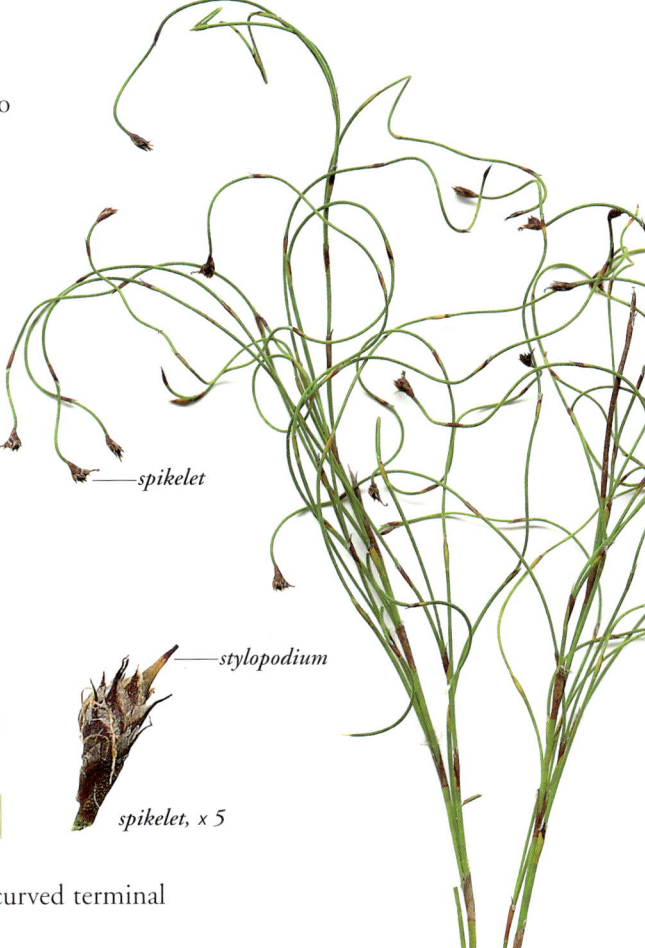

spikelet

stylopodium

spikelet, x 5

Male and Female plants

CULMS branched, with very curved terminal branches, culm surface warty

SHEATHS persistent, body of the sheath pointed, with transparent pointed shoulders (see key, p. 139)

GROWTH FORM low, tightly curled, wiry bushes, up to 20 cm in height, forming a short tangled ground cover

HABITAT amongst rocks and boulders in sandy soils from sea level to mountain plateaux, common to locally dominant

this illustration shows part of a denser plant

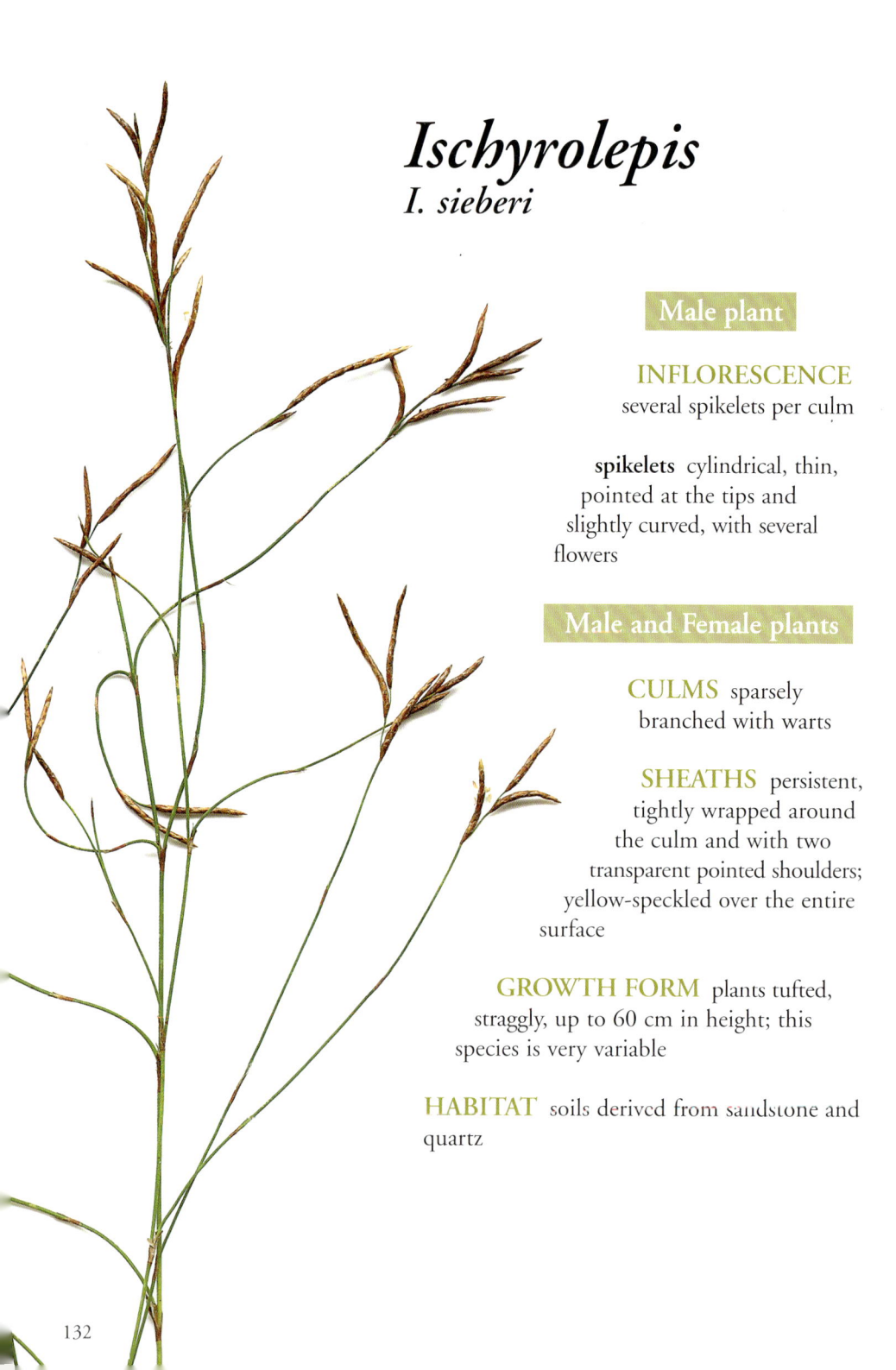

Ischyrolepis
I. sieberi

Male plant

INFLORESCENCE
several spikelets per culm

spikelets cylindrical, thin, pointed at the tips and slightly curved, with several flowers

Male and Female plants

CULMS sparsely branched with warts

SHEATHS persistent, tightly wrapped around the culm and with two transparent pointed shoulders; yellow-speckled over the entire surface

GROWTH FORM plants tufted, straggly, up to 60 cm in height; this species is very variable

HABITAT soils derived from sandstone and quartz

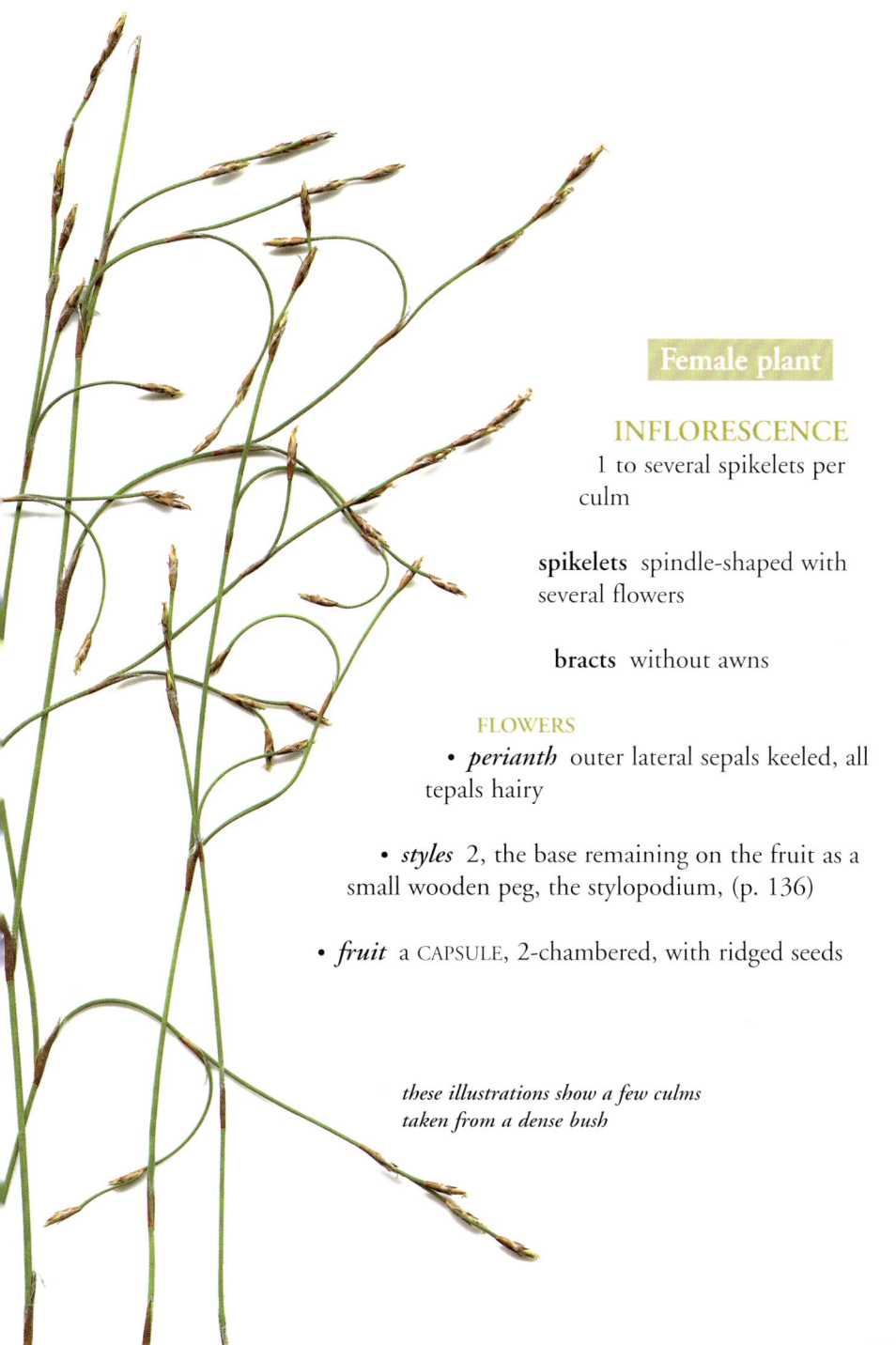

Ischyrolepis

Female plant

INFLORESCENCE
1 to several spikelets per culm

spikelets spindle-shaped with several flowers

bracts without awns

FLOWERS
- *perianth* outer lateral sepals keeled, all tepals hairy

- *styles* 2, the base remaining on the fruit as a small wooden peg, the stylopodium, (p. 136)

- *fruit* a CAPSULE, 2-chambered, with ridged seeds

these illustrations show a few culms taken from a dense bush

young shoot

134

Ischyrolepis
I. subverticellata

Male plant

INFLORESCENCE several to many spikelets on each branch

spikelets slender, spindle-shaped, often slightly curved, with many flowers each

Male and Female plants

CULMS branches in whorls at the nodes along the culms; this particular feature is only known in 4 species of Restionaceae

SHEATH persistent

GROWTH FORM plants tufted on a short rhizome, reaching a height of about 2.5 m and growing in clumps of more than 1 m in diameter

HABITAT a common plant often in semi-shade, along streams, from sea level to the lower mountain slopes

DISTRIBUTION from Paarl to Caledon; absent from the Cape Peninsula

On the older flowers, when the free parts of the 2 styles have withered away, the joined bases remain on the fruit (the capsule) as a persistent peg or **stylopodium** (see also p. 131)

stylopodium

spikelet, x 3.5

Ischyrolepis
I. subverticellata

Female plant

INFLORESCENCE 1-2 spikelets at the tip of the branches

spikelets with 1 or 2 flowers each

FLOWERS
- *styles* 2, joined at the base

- *fruit* a CAPSULE, 2-chambered

spikelet, x 3.5

—— *spikelet*

Ischyrolepis

			♂ spikelets 10-15mm long	
SPIKELETS with 1 or 2 flowers only	CULMS with warts	terminal BRANCHES slightly curved or straight	♂ spikelets 4-10 mm long	
		terminal BRANCHES very curved		
	Body of SHEATHS more or less pointed, with 2 transparent pointed shoulders CULMS with big warts	terminal BRANCHES very curved		

Ischyrolepis

15 Peninsula species, 48 species in total

I. pratensis plants with rhizomes, forming tussocks up to 2 m across	HABITAT sand or gravel, in seasonally wet areas DISTRIBUTION coastal forelands and in valleys from Worcester to the Cape Peninsula
I. curviramis plants long and straggly, seeds warty	HABITAT shallow sand over rock, in slight seepages DISTRIBUTION mountains from Clanwilliam to Swellendam and the Cape Peninsula
I. sporadica plants tufted on rhizomes, seeds net-veined, finely pitted	HABITAT seasonally wet sand, sometimes gravel DISTRIBUTION coastal forelands or mountainous areas between Malmesbury and Bredasdorp
I. cincinnata	HABITAT sandflats on mountains DISTRIBUTION mostly on the Cape Peninsula, some collections from Hermanus and Riviersonderend
I. cincinnata plants forming a low bushy ground cover	

• Species in shaded block is fully illustrated on p. 130

Ischyrolepis

continued from p 139

	Body of the SHEATHS more or less pointed	terminal BRANCHES straight or curved		♀ SPIKELETS sometimes with 3 flowers
		CULMS sparsely branched		
SPIKELETS with 1 or 2 flowers each		terminal BRANCHES very curved	Usually 1 spikelet per culm	SPIKELETS 2-5 mm long
	CULMS with very fine warts, wrinkled or smooth	terminal BRANCHES not curved	several to many spikelets per culm FLOWERS with style bases not joined	♂ SPIKELETS with several flowers

seeds of I. subverticellata, *x 10*

140

Ischyrolepis

15 Peninsula species, 48 species in total

I. eleocharis plants with deep seated black, shiny rhizomes	HABITAT stabilised sand dunes, sometimes on sandy riverbanks, often forming extensive mats DISTRIBUTION from Cape Town to East London
I. cincinnata perianth with 6 hairy tepals	HABITAT see p. 139
I. tenuissima perianth with 4 hairless tepals	HABITAT along streams, on rock flushes and marshes in the mountains DISTRIBUTION from Koue Bokkeveld near Ceres to Piketberg, the Cape Peninsula and Swellendam
I. paludosa culm bases swollen, and reddish seeds with small, smooth bumps	HABITAT swampy or marshy areas, from coastal flats up to 1200 m DISTRIBUTION from the Koue Bokkeveld and Piketberg to the Cape Peninsula and the Bredasdorp flats

culm with pointed sheaths

Ischyrolepis

SPIKELETS with several to many flowers	SHEATHS loosely wrapped around the culms, or flat		BRACTS without awns	SPIKELETS ca. 4 mm long	
			BRACTS with awns	SPIKELETS ca. 10 mm long	CULMS with warts
				SPIKELETS up to 20 mm	CULMS smooth or wrinkled
	SHEATHS tightly wrapped around the culms		BRACTS with or without awns	♂ SPIKELETS curved, cylindrical	
		SHEATHS yellow speckled over the entire surface	BRACTS without awns	♂ spikelets	CULMS with warts —sheath

142

Ischyrolepis

15 Peninsula species, 48 species in total

I. gaudichaudiana plants much branched	HABITAT dry rocky areas DISTRIBUTION from Clanwilliam to Humansdorp
I. capensis	HABITAT dry habitats and disturbed places, at lower altitudes DISTRIBUTION from Ceres to the Cape Peninsula and on to Port Elizabeth
I. ocreata plants sparsely branched	HABITAT dry places DISTRIBUTION mostly in the western part of the Cape, common in the Cederberg
I. triflora	HABITAT clayey soils derived from shale or granite (grassy fynbos or renosterveld) DISTRIBUTION from Paarl to the Cape Peninsula and on to Grahamstown
I. sieberi plants straggly, up to 60 cm in height seeds ridged, species very variable	HABITAT well-drained slopes and among rocks, frequently dominating the vegetation after fire DISTRIBUTION widespread from Namaqualand and Richtersveld to Grahamstown

• *Species in shaded block are fully illustrated on pp. 128, 132*

Restio
R. egregius

Male plant

INFLORESCENCE several to many spikelets per culm, with small spathes

spikelets pendulous, with 2 to many flowers

bracts slightly longer than the flowers

Male and Female plants

CULMS stout, sparsely branched

SHEATHS persistent

GROWTH FORM tufted but rather tangled bushes up to 1 m in height, growing in loose tussocks; plants resprout after fire

HABITAT mountains and hilly places, most common below 1000 m, widespread in the Cape of Good Hope Nature Reserve

Restio

Female plant

INFLORESCENCE
1-2 spikelets per culm, with small spathes

spikelets with 2 to many flowers

bracts slightly longer than the flowers, firm, tapering to a sharp awn

spathes small

FLOWERS flattened
- *perianth* 10 mm long, lateral sepals smooth, not keeled

- *styles* 3

- *fruit* a CAPSULE, 2-chambered

flowers

Restio
R. dispar

Male plant

INFLORESCENCE many spikelets per culm, overtopped by the spathes

spikelets with several flowers each

bracts papery

Male and Female plants

CULMS slightly branched and sparsely warty

SHEATHS persistent, tightly wrapped around the culm

GROWTH FORM plants tufted, forming bushes up to 2 m in height

HABITAT along streams and among rocks in the mountains

Restio

Female plant

INFLORESCENCE several spikelets per culm, overtopped by long, maroon-red spathes, a distinctive feature of the female plants of this species

spikelets with several flowers each

bracts papery

FLOWERS flattened
- *perianth* lateral sepals keeled

- *styles* 3

- *fruit* a CAPSULE, 1-chambered

spikelet inside spathe

Restio
R. tetragonus

Restio

young plant, not yet flowering

Male and Female plants

INFLORESCENCES
similar, except for the flowers

FEMALE FLOWERS
- *perianth* lateral sepals hairy

- *styles* 3

- *fruit* a CAPSULE, 3-chambered

GROWTH FORM plants tufted, reaching a height of 1.5 m, with graceful, light green, fine, silky-soft feathery branches; rather similar (but shorter) in appearance to *Calopsis paniculata* (p. 122) but easy to distinguish by their square (4-angled) culms

HABITAT shales or clayey soil, along the foothills of coastal mountains, often in cool and damp places

square culm

Restio

CULMS square (4-angled)	SPIKELETS 6-8 mm long			FLOWERS with lateral sepals hairy
	SPIKELETS 4-6 mm long	SPIKELETS x 3.5		FLOWERS with lateral sepals hairless

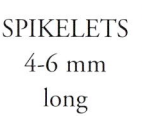

CULMS round in cross-section	CAPSULES with 3 chambers

best seen on older flowers, where the capsules have split open

the 3 styles are usually central on the ovary | SPIKELETS with few to many flowers x 3.5 | | SHEATHS with long linear awns |
| | | | | FLOWERS smaller than the bracts

BRACTS pointed |

150

Restio

21 Peninsula species, 90 species in total

R. tetragonus plants 60-100 cm tall	HABITAT shaly or clayey soil DISTRIBUTION along foothills of coastal mountains between Cape Town and Humansdorp
R. quadratus plants 150-200 cm tall	HABITAT damp places, stream banks or seepages, often on shaly or granite soils DISTRIBUTION from Paarl to Bredasdorp
R. quinquefarius	HABITAT sandy flats in dry areas, mostly at sea level but in the Cederberg at 1000 m DISTRIBUTION between Clanwilliam and Cape Point
R. pedicellatus	HABITAT marshy areas or on rock flushes DISTRIBUTION from the Cederberg to the Piketberg, the Cape Peninsula and Caledon

• *Species in shaded block is fully illustrated on p. 148*

R. quinquefarius, x 3.5

Restio

CULMS round in cross-section	*capsules, x 2* CAPSULES with 2 chambers, both fertile, 1 sometimes aborted *best seen on older flowers where the capsules have split open*	SPIKELETS with 1-2 flowers	FLOWERS with lateral sepals hairy		
			FLOWERS with lateral sepals hairless	BRACTS shorter than the flowers and lacerated	
		SPIKELETS with few to many flowers	*flower, x 2*	BRACTS equal to or slightly longer than the flowers	

Restio

21 Peninsula species, 90 species in total

CULMS more or less warty	*R. perplexus*	HABITAT quite common, often found amongst rocks in the mountains DISTRIBUTION from Ceres to the Cape Peninsula and to Riversdale
	R. sejunctus	HABITAT rocky slopes, from 900-1800 m DISTRIBUTION from Paarl to the Natal Drakensberg
CULMS unbranched	*R. pedicellatus*	HABITAT marshy areas or rock flushes in the mountains DISTRIBUTION see p. 151
lower half of the SHEATHS red-brown	*R. ambiguus*	HABITAT marshy areas DISTRIBUTION from the Cape Peninsula to the mountains at Genadendal and south to Hermanus
tepals of flowers 10 mm long	*R. egregius* *open flower, x 2*	HABITAT mountain slopes and hillsides, most common below 1000 m DISTRIBUTION from the Cape Peninsula to Villiersdorp and Bredasdorp
tepals of flowers 4-6 mm long	*R. micans*	HABITAT in moist depressions in sand, very local at sea level along the coastal forelands DISTRIBUTION from Malmesbury to the Cape Flats

• *Species in shaded block is fully illustrated on p. 144*

Restio

| CULMS round in cross-section | CAPSULES with 2 chambers, both fertile, 1 sometimes aborted *best seen on older flowers where the capsules have split open* | *capsules* SPIKELETS with few to many flowers *spikelet, x 2* **R. bifidus** | x 3.5 FLOWERS with hairs on the ridged lateral sepals x 3.5 | BRACTS rounded with a short stiff awn x 3.5 BRACTS lacerated and ciliate BRACTS almost flat with purple-brown bands on the side of the awn BRACTS pointed with smooth margins |

Restio

21 Peninsula species, 90 species in total

CULMS sparsely branched or unbranched, flattened or slightly ridged and wrinkled	*R. bifurcus* *flowers, x 2*	HABITAT sandy soils DISTRIBUTION from Malmesbury to the Cape Peninsula and Shaw's Mountain
CULMS much branched	*R. multiflorus* (variable species)	HABITAT scattered in rocky places DISTRIBUTION mountains of the south-western Cape, from the Piketberg to Bredasdorp
CULMS much branched, diam. < 1 mm at the base	*R. communis*	HABITAT marshy areas DISTRIBUTION only on the Cape Peninsula, at Cape Point and Silvermine
CULMS sparsely branched or unbranched	*R. bifidus* *flower, x 3.5*	HABITAT seepages and wet areas DISTRIBUTION from the Cape Peninsula to Jonkershoek and Hermanus
	R. filiformis	HABITAT dry stony mountain slopes DISTRIBUTION widespread and common, from Clanwilliam to the Cape Peninsula on to Riversdale

Restio

CULMS round in cross-section	CAPSULES with 1 chamber only, with 1 seed *best seen on older flowers where the capsule is split open* the 3 styles are excentric on the ovary	SPIKELETS with 2 to many flowers	FLOWERS with lateral sepals winged on upper half of middle ridge	FLOWERS with lateral sepals equal
				FLOWERS with lateral sepals unequal, lacerated
			FLOWERS with lateral sepals not winged	SPIKELETS slender, spindle-shaped slightly curved
				SPATHES longer than the spikelets and maroon red
				SPATHES shorter than the spikelets

Restio

21 Peninsula species, 90 species in total

	R. distichus	HABITAT dry, often gravelly mountain slopes DISTRIBUTION Cederberg to the Great Swartberg and the Cape Peninsula (not on the Outeniqua and Tsitsikamma Mountains)
	R. dodii	HABITAT low altitude marshes DISTRIBUTION on the Cape Peninsula at Cape Point, and the Bredasdorp flats
CULMS with dense flat-topped whitish warts	*R. triticeus*	HABITAT widespread in dry fynbos, often on conglomerate soils DISTRIBUTION from Cape Town to the Transkei, very common in the Southern Cape
CULMS smooth or with very fine warts	*R. dispar*	HABITAT along streams and among rocks DISTRIBUTION mountains from Bainskloof to the Cape Peninsula and Bredasdorp
	R. leptostachyus lateral sepals, hairless	HABITAT rocky slopes at higher altitudes DISTRIBUTION Cape Peninsula and the higher mountains from Du Toits Kloof to Riviersonderend
	R. sarocladus lateral, hairy sepals; plants with long rhizomes	HABITAT from sea level to 1000 m DISTRIBUTION Cape Peninsula and the coastal mountains of the Caledon district

• Species in shaded block is fully illustrated on p. 146

Platycaulos
P. major

Male plant

INFLORESCENCE several spikelets per culm with small spathes

spikelets more than 2.5 cm long, with 1 to several flowers each

bracts papery, longer than the flowers

Male and Female plants

CULMS branched, more or less flattened

SHEATHS persistent, green (particularly on the young parts of the culm), with long, stout awns

GROWTH FORM tangled bushes, up to 60 cm in height

HABITAT damp places and seepages in mountains and along streams

DISTRIBUTION from the Cape Peninsula to Humansdorp

The genus *Platycaulos* contains 8 species in total. The only other species found on the Cape Peninsula is *P. compressus;* it is very similar to *P. major,* except for the size of the female spikelets, which are shorter than 2.5 cm; it occupies the same habitat and has the same distribution range

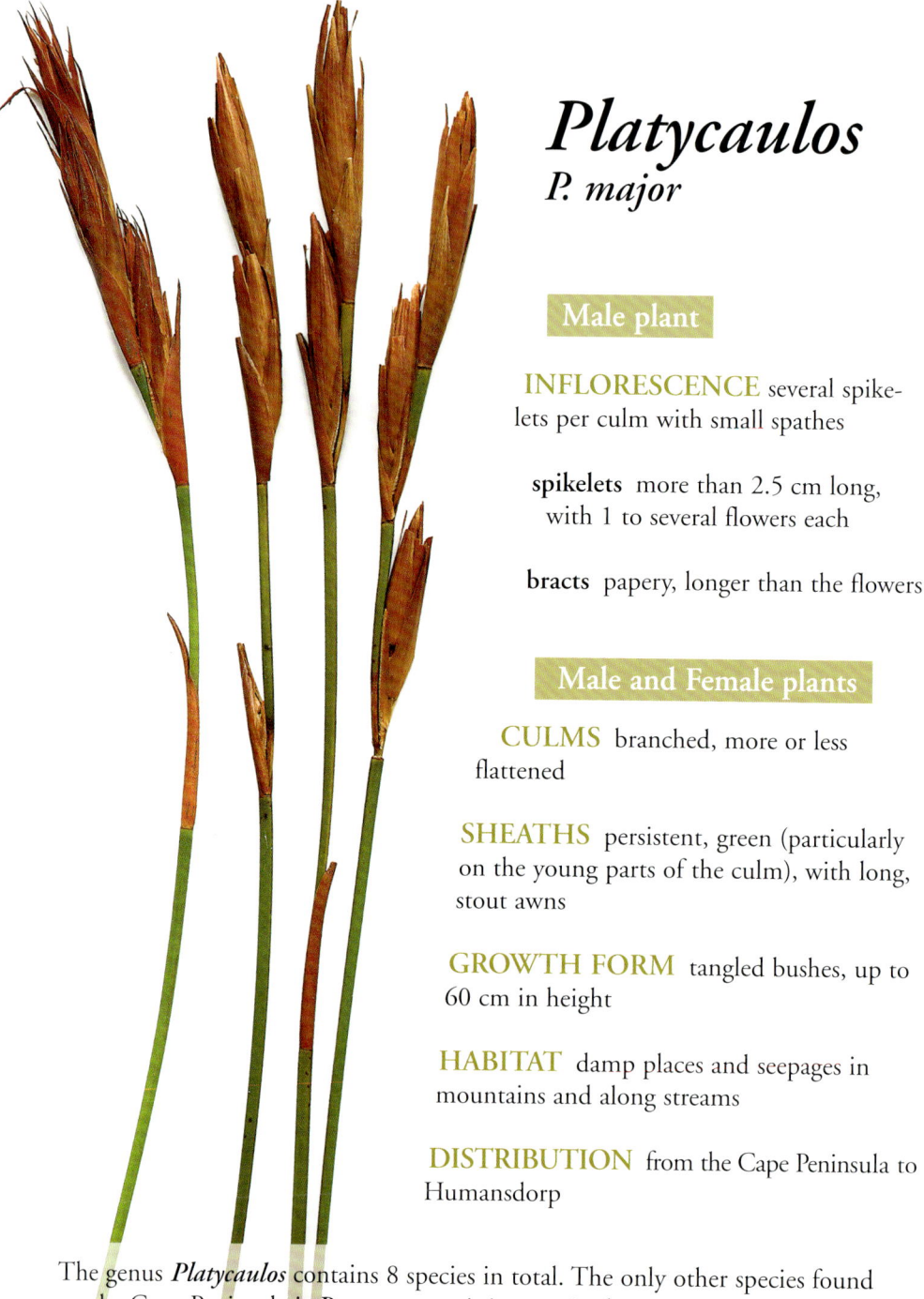

Platycaulos

Female plant

INFLORESCENCE several spikelets per culm with small spathes

spikelets similar but somewhat bigger than those of the male, with 1 to several flowers each

bracts papery, longer than the flowers

FLOWERS flattened
- *perianth* tepals bony, lateral sepals keeled

- *styles* 3, feathery

- *fruit* a CAPSULE, 1-3 chambered, with white, ornamented seeds

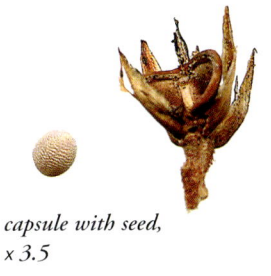

capsule with seed, x 3.5

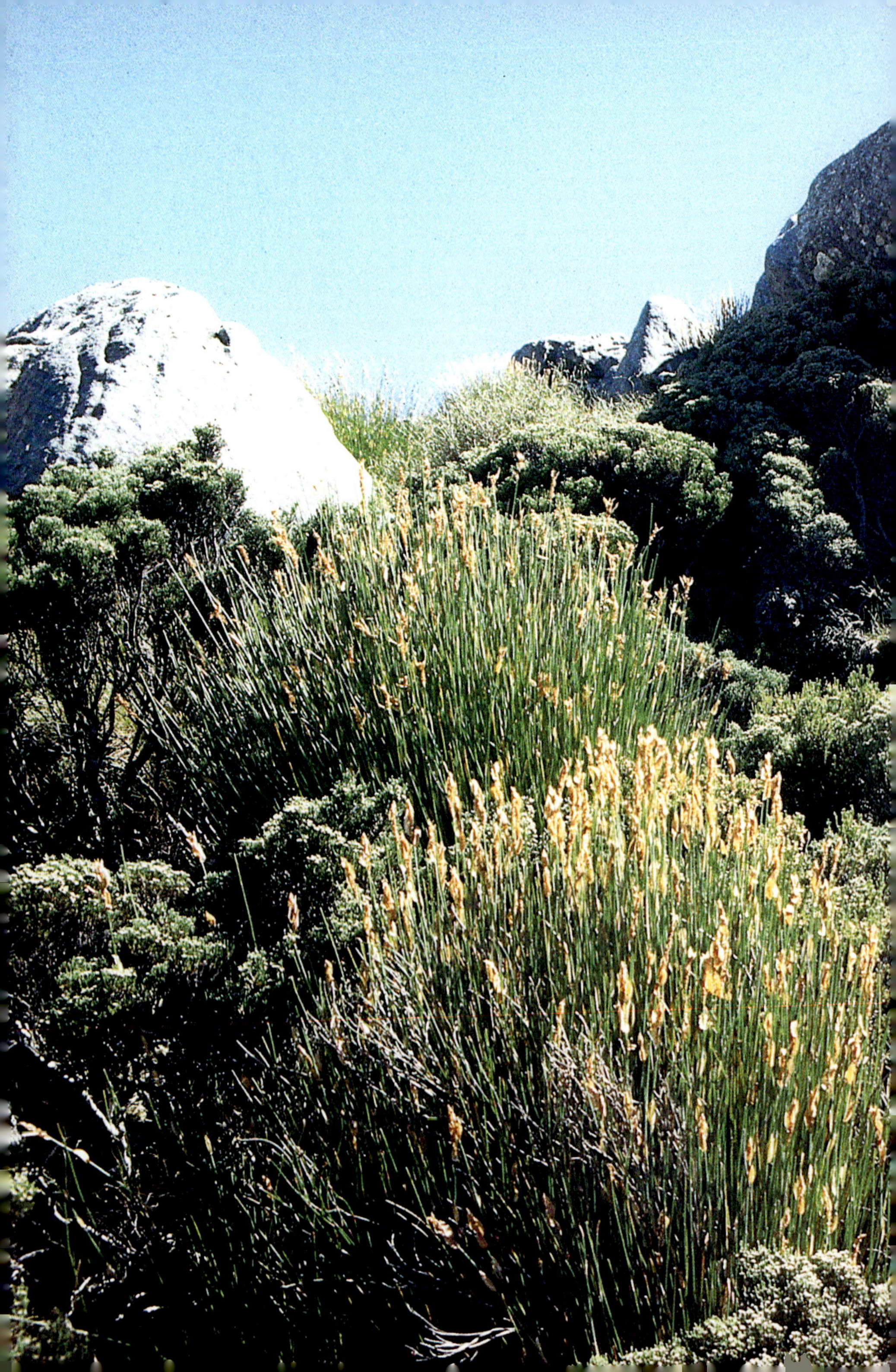

GROWING RESTIOS

... and having seen the restios in all their splendour in the fynbos, imagine their beauty in your garden ...

Introduction

With the threat of an ever increasing water shortage in South Africa many gardeners and landscape architects have, over the last ten years, been looking for indigenous plants which are well adapted to drought conditions and could be used for water-wise gardening. In the Cape this meant turning to fynbos plants.

Cultivated by many nurseries numerous attractive, well-known fynbos plants like proteas, ericas and geophytes slowly made their entry into domestic gardens. Whilst restios were not excluded from this group and a small number of species became quite popular, many very attractive species could not be cultivated because their seeds and nuts were almost impossible to germinate.

However, after years of experimenting by horticulturists, Hannes de Lange (a research scientist at the National Botanical Institute in Cape Town) discovered that smoke derived from fynbos fire is a natural stimulant to the germination of many fynbos plants.

Further smoke trials on restio seeds by Hanneke Jamieson (a horticulturist at Kirstenbosch National Botanical Garden) proved successful too, and the horticultural potential of the restios is now firmly established.

Thamnochortus fruticosus

growing restios

A beautiful Restio Garden now graces Kirstenbosch, designed and developed for display and used for ongoing research in the cultivation of the Restionaceae.

Els Dorrat Haaksma under the Cannomois virgata *in Kirstenbosch Garden*

An increasing number of species is becoming available and it looks as though the demand for Restionaceae in garden and landscape plantings will grow substantially in the coming years.

Although restios do not offer the great splashes of colour they have many other attractive features which make them desirable plants for the garden:

- Restios come in many elegant shapes and textures, with colours ranging from delicate greys and greens to shades of bronze, russet and golden browns. Some have spectacular sculptural features. Either as single accent plants, or planted in groups, their unusual features will greatly enhance the garden, especially as a complement to other fynbos plants.

- Several species can be grown in pots.

- Many species are excellent as cutting material for fresh or dried flower arrangements.

- Even with very little water they still maintain colour and shape throughout the dry season, and as such serve as wonderful permanent features in water-wise gardens.

- They are particularly resilient to strong winds and heavy rain.

- The plants require little maintenance, which makes them suitable for permanent public plantings, cutting down on maintenance costs. With their planting requirements met they will be virtually disease free.

- Planting the indigenous restios is ecologically sensible and will make your garden truly complete.

growing restios

♀

♂

Thamnochortus
cinereus

165

Planting Restios

RESTIO REQUIREMENTS
Restios need **full sun.** Only a few species can tolerate partial or light shade, but all will do better in full sun.

All restios need an open position with plenty of **air movement.**

Restios will grow in almost any kind of **well-drained soil**. They grow best in acid soil.

The only known species tolerating alkaline soils are *Elegia filacea, Chondropetalum tectorum, Thamnochortus pellucidus* and *Thamnochortus insignis.*

PLANTING
- The best time to plant a restio is at the beginning of the rainy season.

- Dig a hole of 0.5 m square and deep.

- Remove weeds and mix the excavated soil with two spadesful of well rotted compost.

- Wet the plant thoroughly in the bag before taking it out.

- Put the plant into the hole and add the soil mixture to the same level as it was in the bag.

growing restios

MAINTENANCE

- Water well (every second day) for the first three months (in the absence of good rains). After this your plants will welcome some water once a week, but can survive on very little. With more watering they will grow greener and more lush and will retain their juvenile foliage longer.

- Feed regularly with a liquid organic fertiliser or a slow release fertiliser which is low in phosphate.

- Mulch with composted pine bark or rough compost.

- Do not unnecessarily disturb the roots.
  The plants do not like being waterlogged or having competition from lawn grass around them.

Restios, once established, look after themselves. They need neither extra water nor feeding and will give years of carefree beauty to the garden. Some species (e.g. *Thamnochortus insignis*) have a life span of up to thirty years.

New shoots will be produced each year, and the only maintenance, after three years, is to remove the dead (brown) culms at the end of the growing season, when the new culms have reached their full height.

As long as they have a good open position in the ground with plenty of air around them they will be virtually disease free.

The following pages list a selected number of species which are usually stocked by nurseries.

A selection of available species

SMALL PLANTS	maximum height	maximum spread	planting distance
Elegia filacea	0.5 m	0.25 m	0.3 m
Elegia stipularis	0.5 m	0.3 m	0.3 m
Thamnochortus pellucidus	0.6 m	0.5 m	0.4 m
Chondropetalum ebracteatum	0.6 m	0.5 m	0.7 m

Elegia stipularis *in Kirstenbosch Garden*

growing restios

illustrated on page:	GARDENING NOTES	
54	Elegant slender plant; suitable for containers	Plant in groups of at least 5 for best effect in the garden
56, 168, 169	Plant for colour effect; tolerates sea wind with salt and sand; suitable for containers	
176	Tolerates sea wind with salt and sand, and alkaline soil; suitable for containers	
26, 48	Elegant slender plant; attractive as a single specimen in open garden or rockery; suitable for containers	

Elegia stipularis

A selection of available species (ctd)

MEDIUM-SIZED PLANTS	maximum height	spread	planting distance
Rhodocoma capensis	0.9 m	0.6 m	0.6 m
Thamnochortus lucens	0.9 m	0.6 m	0.7 m
Elegia cuspidata	1 m	0.8 m	1 m
Thamnochortus cinereus	1 m	0.8 m	0.8 m

Rhodocoma capensis *(in centre)*

Thamnochortus lucens

Chondropetalum tectorum	1.5 m	1 m	1 m
Elegia racemosa	1.5 m	1 m	1 m

growing restios

illustrated on page:	GARDENING NOTES	
92, 170	Attractive dark green bushy plants	Plant in groups or use as accent plants
74, 170	Graceful, elegant plant with pale-bronze flowerheads	
60	Spreading plant with striking chestnut coloured spathes and sheaths; use as accent plant next to soft greens	
165	Bushy plant with silver flower heads; tolerates sea wind with salt and sand; suitable for containers	

Chondropetalum tectorum

46, 171	Tolerates sea wind with salt and sand, copes with frost and can grow in alkaline soil; suitable for containers; lifespan ca.10 years; use in small groups or as accent plant
26, 60	Attractive plant with beautiful golden flowerheads; use as accent plant

A selection of available species (ctd)

TALL PLANTS	maximum height	spread	planting distance
Thamnochortus insignis	2 m	3 m	2-3 m
Restio quadratus *Restio tetragonus*	2 m 1.8 m	2 m	1-2 m
Elegia capensis	2 m	1.5 m	2 m

Thamnochortus insignis

Restio tetragonus

Ischyrolepis subverticellata	2 m	0.7 m	1.5 m
Rhodocoma gigantea	2.5 m	1 m	1 m
Calopsis paniculata	3 m	1.5 m	2-3 m

growing restios

illustrated on page:	GARDENING NOTES
84, 172	Striking plant; tolerates sea wind with salt and sand, and alkaline soil; can cope with frost; life span ca.30 years
148, 172	Sumptuous spreading plants with luscious soft-green feathery foliage; species similar
x, 62	Very sculptural spreading plant forming big tussocks; quick growing; has been in cultivation for a long time

Ischyrolepis subverticellata

Rhodocoma gigantea
in a private garden

134, 136, 173	Graceful spreading plant forming big tussocks; tolerates sea wind with salt and sand; can grow in light shade; has been in cultivation for over 100 years
173	Erect plant with masses of bright green foliage
27, 122	Spreading plant, with arching branches; forms big tussocks; tolerates light shade; good at water's edge (its natural habitat)

Propagation

Restios can be propagated in two different ways: either by division of the rhizomes or by seed (seeds and nuts).

A. DIVIDING THE RHIZOME

The best time to divide rhizomatous species is in early winter, before the new culms arise from the rhizome.

- Break the rhizome into fairly big pieces and plant them straight away (before they dry out) into the ground or in pots. Take care not to disturb the roots too much.

- Water the new plants until new shoots emerge from the rhizome. This can take at least half a year. Keep the divided plants under light shade.

Cannomois parviflora

growing restios

B. SOWING SEED (seeds, nuts and nutlets)

Growing plants from seed has the advantage of producing many more plants at a time than by dividing them. The plants seem to be happier and grow bigger when established from seedlings than from pieces of rhizome. However for successful germination most seeds and nuts need smoke treatment.

A smoke tent

There are 2 ways of applying the smoke:

1. Soaking the seeds for 24 hours in a solution of 'Kirstenbosch Smoke Plus' seed primer before sowing them.

2. Using a smoke tent (see illustration above). Sow your seeds in seed trays (see p. 176). Lead the smoke generated from a small fire from plant material through this tent for half an hour, then leave the tray to stand for another half an hour.

Seeds and nuts of a good number of species are available. For information on nurseries which sell restio seed please consult the advertisements in *Veld & Flora* (the Botanical Society of South Africa's magazine).

Propagation (ctd)

HOW TO RAISE PLANTS from SEED
(seeds, nuts and nutlets)

Smoke Treatment
Choose either one of the two smoke treatments as discussed on p. 175.

Sowing Time
The ideal time to sow is early autumn, i.e. when day and night temperatures fluctuate between ca. 22 °C and 10 °C.

Sowing Medium
Use an acid mixture of loam, fine composted milled bark and coarse sand, (1:2:2) or premixed fynbos soil. Cover seeds with a thin layer of milled bark and keep moist, watering at least once a day. Use smoke-tent treatment at this stage if seeds are not presoaked.

Germination Time
Seeds will take 3-4 weeks to germinate.

Pricking Out
About six weeks after germination when the first three small stems have developed, prick out individual seedlings into half litre bags or pots containing well drained soil and add a slow release fertiliser.

Keep the seedlings moist at all times for the next six months.

Thamnochortus pellucidus, *similar to* T. lucens, *but smaller*

growing restios

Planting out in the garden

The growth rate of the different species varies greatly. Most species will be at least 60 cm tall after the growth flush of early summer and will be big enough to be planted out in the garden.

Some smaller seedlings will only start growing well once they have been planted out in the garden. They will all reach their full height about four years after germination.

Flowering Time

About two years after planting some species have a few flowering culms but most species will only start flowering in the third year. Over the next few years the number of flowering culms will increase (see also p. 11).

The young plants of some species (e.g *Elegia cuspidata*) look very different from the mature plants.

Thamnochortus sp. with juvenile 'foliage' at the base

Juvenile Foliage

During the first six months of growth plants of many species produce a bushy kind of growth at the base. Later, once they have flowered, this growth can also appear at the nodes along the culms. This growth consists of small sterile culms, which horticulturists often refer to as 'foliage' (see illustration above).

Glossary for the Restionaceae

Illustrations to all these botanical terms can be found in the MORPHOLOGY section, on pp. 25-41

anther	part of the male reproductive organ (stamen) that contains the pollen grains	foliage	a term used by horticulturists to describe the juvenile (sterile) growth and densely branched parts of restio plants
awn	a stiff bristle-like projection from the tip of the bract or sheath	genus	a taxonomic group consisting of closely related species
bract	a modified leaf	inflorescence	that part of the main culm or branch which carries the spikelet(s); in layman's terms often called flowerhead
calyx	the outer whorl of tepals of a flower, surrounding the corolla		
capsule	a dry fruit which splits open when ripe to release the seeds	keel	folded part of a sepal
ciliate	with a fringe of hairs at the margin	locule	a seed chamber of a capsule holding one seed only
corolla	the inner whorl of petals of a flower	margin	edge
culm	the stem of restios, grasses and sedges	morphology	the study of the shape or form of the external structure of organisms
dimorphism	having two shapes	nut	a big (up to 10 mm) one-seeded fruit with a hard, woody (ovary) wall, not splitting open when ripe to release the seed
dioecious	plants of separate sexes, i.e. plants bearing either only male or only female flowers		
endemic	growing in one particular place only	nutlet	a small (< 5 mm) one-seeded fruit with a soft (ovary) wall, not splitting open when ripe to release the seed
elaiosome	a fleshy structure on some restio nuts; it comes in various shapes, usually sitting at the base of the nut; a food sought after by ants and instrumental in seed dispersal	ovary	the base of the female reproductive organ of the flower (the gynaecium) which matures into either a nut, nutlet or a capsule
		♂	symbol for male
family	a taxonomic group consisting of closely related genera	♀	symbol for female

panicle	a branched inflorescence	**style**	top part of the female reproductive organ (with a stigmatic surface) picking up the pollen from the air
petal	a floral leaf of the restio flower, part of the inner whorl of 3 tepals		
perianth	the 6 floral leaves, or tepals, of a restio flower, arranged in two whorls of 3 petals and 3 sepals; petals and sepals can be identical	**stylopodium**	the joined bases of the 2 styles of a female *Ischyrolepis* flower, which remain on the capsule as a small woody peg
		tepal	a collective name for the floral leaves of the restio flower, the 3 sepals and 3 petals
rhizome	a horizontally creeping underground stem with roots and covered with brown scale leaves	**tufted**	a growth form which is narrow at the base and wide at the top
sepal	a floral leaf of the restio flower, part of the outer whorl of 3 tepals	**wing**	extended keel of sepal
		whorl	a ring of plant parts (e.g. branches, or tepals) around a stem; in branches successive whorls are usually well separated from each other
sheath	a reduced leaf, i.e. lacking the leaf blade, split to the base and partly enveloping the culm		
spathe	a large bract subtending part of, or ensheathing the whole inflorescence		
spathellae	small spathes in some *Elegia* inflorescences		
species	a taxonomic group (unit) below genus rank; reproductively isolated from other groups, i.e. interbreeding and gene flow occur among members of one species but not usually between members of different species		
spike	a type of inflorescence, consisting of an elongated main axis with bracts and stalkless flowers		
spikelet	a small spike, the basic unit of the restio inflorescence		

Female flower of Restio bifurcus *with 3 tepals removed, showing the large green ovary (with hairlike sterile stamens) and the 3 feathery styles, x 12*

Bibliography

Brown, N.A.C., Jamieson, H. and Hitchcock, A. (1996). Conservation through cultivation. *The Garden, Journal of the Royal Horticultural Society* **121** (5):265-267.

Brown, N.A.C., Jamieson, H., Botha P. (1998). *Grow Restios*. National Botanical Institute, Cape Town.

Cowling, R. and Richardson, D. (1995). *Fynbos*. Fernwood Press, in association with the Institute of Plant Conservation, Cape Town.

De Lange, J.H. and Boucher, C. (1990). Autecological studies on *Audouinia capitata* (Bruniaceae). *I:* plant derived smoke as a seed germination cue. *South African Journal of Botany* **56**, (6), 700-703.

Jamieson, H. and Brown, N.A.C. (1994). The restio garden at Kirstenbosch. *Veld & Flora* **80** (4): 124-125.

Jamieson, H., Hitchcock, A. and Brown N.A.C. (1995). Growing restios. *Veld & Flora* **81** (4): 129-130.

Linder, H.P. (1984). A phylogenetic classification of the genera of the African Restionaceae. *Bothalia* **15**, (1 & 2): 11-76.

Linder, H.P. (1985). Conspectus of the African species of Restionaceae. *Bothalia* **15**, (3 & 4): 387-503.

Linder, H.P. (1991). A review of the Southern African Restionaceae. *Contributions from the Bolus Herbarium* **13**: 209-264.

Linder, H.P. (1992). The structure and evolution of the female flower of the African Restionaceae. *Botanical Journal of the Linnean Society,* **109**: 401-425.

Rourke, J.P. (1974). On restios and roofs. *Veld & Flora* (former series) **4** (3): 57-59.

Slingsby, P. and Bond, W.J. (1981). Ants, friends of the Fynbos. *Veld & Flora* **67** (2): 39-45.

Names of illustrated species

GROWTH FORM pp. 26, 27
1. *Ischyrolepis cincinnata*

RHIZOMES pp. 28, 29
1. *Hypodiscus aristatus*; 2. *Hypodiscus willdenowia*; 3. *Thamnochortus* sp.; 4. *Cannomois parviflora*;
5. *Elegia squamosa*

CULMS pp. 30, 31
1. *Calopsis paniculata*; 2. *Elegia* sp.; 3. *Thamnochortus lucens*; 4. *Ischyrolepis cincinnata*;
5, 6, 7. *Elegia* sp.; 8. *Restio tetragonus*; 9. *Elegia fistulosa*; 10. *Willdenowia incurvata*;
11. *Thamnochortus fruticosa*

SHEATHS pp. 32, 33
1. *Platycaulos major*; 2. *Willdenowia incurvata*; 3. *Chondropetalum ebracteatum*; 4, 5, 6. *Elegia* sp.;
7. *Ischyrolepis capensis*; 8. *Mastersiella digitata*; 9. *Elegia* sp.; 10. *Willdenowia incurvata*; 11. *Calopsis paniculata*; 12. *Anthochortus crinalis*; 13. *Thamnochortus lucens*

INFLORESCENCES pp. 34, 35
1. *Chondropetalum tectorum*; 2. *Chondropetalum ebracteatum*; 3, 4. *Staberoha cernua*; 5. *Ischyrolepis cincinnata*; 6. *Restio quinquefarius*; 7. *Ischyrolepis eleocharis*; 8. *Elegia* sp.;
9. *Hypodiscus aristatus*; 10. *Restio triticeus*; 11. *Willdenowia glomerata*; 12,13. *Thamnochortus lucens*

SPIKELETS pp. 36, 37
1. *Thamnochortus spicigerus*; 2. *Ischyrolepis eleocharis*; 3. *Ischyrolepis subverticellata*; 4. *Ischyrolepis cincinnata*; 5. *Thamnochortus* sp.; 6. *Restio quinquefarius*; 7. *Ischyrolepis capensis*; 8. *Hypodiscus aristatus*;
9. *Mastersiella digitata*; 10. *Willdenowia incurvata*; 11. *Hypodiscus willdenowia*; 12. *Ceratocaryum argenteum*; 13. *Restio dispar*; 14. *Hypodiscus aristatus*; 15,16. *Staberoha banksii*; 17. *Elegia racemosa*;
18, 19. *Chondropetalum tectorum*; 20. *Elegia* sp.; 21. *Cannomois virgata*; 22. *Ischyrolepis capensis*;
23. *Askidiosperma paniculatum*

FLOWERS pp. 38, 39
1. *Nevillea obtusissima*; 2. *Hypodiscus willdenowia*; 3,4. *Ischyrolepis subverticellata*; 5. *Chondropetalum tectorum*; 6. *Hypodiscus aristatus*; 7. *Ischyrolepis sieberi*; 8. *Anthochortus crinalis*; 9. *Chondropetalum microcarpum*; 10, 11. *Staberoha* sp.; 12. *Thamnochortus lucens*; 13. *Elegia fistulosa*; 14. *Hypodiscus willdenowia*; 15. *Willdenowia glomerata*; 16. *Chondropetalum tectorum*; 17. *Ceratocaryum argenteum*;
18. *Chondropetalum mucronatum*; 19. *Elegia fistulosa*; 20. *Willdenowia teres*; 21. *Restio bifidus*;
22. *Restio bifurcus*; 23. *Thamnochortus lucens*; 24. *Thamnochortus* sp.; 25. *Thamnochortus insignis*

NUTS and CAPSULES pp. 40, 41
1. *Mastersiella digitata*; 2. *Cannomois virgata*; 3. *Platycaulos major*; 4. *Dovea macrocarpa*;
5. *Chondropetalum tectorum*; 6. *Restio quinquefarius*; 7. *Restio dispar*; 8. *Willdenowia glomerata*;
9. *Hypodiscus willdenowia*; 10. *Hypodiscus aristatus*; 11. *Elegia filacea*; 12. *Willdenowia teres*;
13. *Willdenowia sulcata*; 14. *Hypodiscus albo-aristatus*; 15. *Willdenowia teres*; 16. *Thamnochortus lucens*

Index

Figures printed in bold refer to illustrations of the species. The main illustrations of male and female plants are mentioned first.

Anarthria 18

Anthochortus Nees 18, 19, 42, 112
 capensis Esterhuysen 113
 crinalis (Mast.) Linder 110, 112, 113, 5, 15, 27, 33(12), 38(8)
 laxiflorus (Nees) Linder 113

Apodasmia chilensis 3

Askidiosperma Steud. 19, 42
 paniculatum (Mast.) Linder 70, 37(23)

Calopsis Desv. 9, 18, 19, 42, 126
 fruticosa (Mast.) Linder 127
 gracilis (Mast.) Linder 127
 membranacea (Pillans) Linder 127
 paniculata (Rottb.) Desv. 122, 125, 127, 27, 30(1) 33(11), 149, 172
 viminea (Rottb.) Linder 124, 127

Cannomois Desv. 10, 18, 19, 42
 nitida (Mast.) Pillans 15
 taylori Linder 16
 parviflora (Thunb.) Pillans 120, 29(4) 174
 virgata (Rottb.) Steud. 116, 118, 37(21), 40(2), 163

Cephalelenii 12

Ceratocaryum Nees 10, 18, 19, 42
 argenteum Nees ex Kunth 102, 8, 36(12), 39(17)

Chondropetalum Rottb. 19, 42, 46, 52, 71, 73
 deustum Rottb. 53
 ebracteum (Kunth) Pillans 48, 52, 53, 26, 32(3), 34(2), 168

microcarpum (Kunth) Pillans 5, 38(9), 52, 53
mucronatum (Nees) Pillans 50, 52, 53, 39(18)
nudum Rottb. 52, 53, 53
rectum (Mast.) Pillans 53
tectorum (L.f.) Rafin. 46, 52, 53, 7, 11, 16, 34(1), 37(18,19), 38(5), 39(16), 40(5), 166, 170, 171

Chrysomelid bug 12

Disa 3

Dovea Kunth 19, 42
 macrocarpa Kunth 72, 40(4)

Ecdeiocolea 18

Elegia L. 8, 19, 42, 30(2,5,6,7), 32(4,5,6) 33(9), 34(8), 37(20), 64, 66, 68, 71, 73
 amoena Pillans 4
 asperiflora (Nees) Kunth 67
 capensis (Burm. f.) Schelpe 62, 63, 64, 65, viii, 42, 172
 coleura Nees ex Mast. 67
 cuspidata Mast. 60, 68, 69, 5, 170,177
 fenestrata Pillans 58, 69
 filacea Mast. 54, 67, 5, 13, 40(11), 57, 166, 168
 fistulosa Kunth 60, 66, 67, 31(9), 38(13), 39(19)
 grandispicata Linder 5
 intermedia (Steud.) Pilllans 61, 69
 juncea L. 69
 neesii Mast. 65
 persistens Mast. 61
 prominens Pillans 65
 racemosa (Poir.) Pers. 60, 69, 26, 37(17), 170

182

spathacea Mast. 5
squamosa Mast. **29**(5), 67
stipularis Mast. **56**, **65**, **168**, **169**
thyrsifera (Rottb.) Pers. 69
vaginulata Mast. 67
verreauxii Mast. 67

Erica 3

Grasses 22, 18

Hopkinsia 18

Hydrophilus Linder 18, 19, 42
  rattrayi (Pillans) Linder **114**

Hypodiscus Nees **10**, 18,19, 42, 98
  albo-aristatus (Nees) Mast. **99**, 98, **41**(14)
  argenteus (Thunb.) Mast. 98
  aristatus (Thunb.) Krauss **94**, 10, 26, **28**(1), **35**(9), **36**(8), **37**(14), **38**(6), **40**(10)
  montanus Esterhuysen 3
  rugosus Mast. 98
  striatus (Kunth) Mast. 7
  willdenowia (Nees) Mast. **96**, 98, 7, **28**(2), **36**(11), **38**(2, 14), **40**(9), 98

Hyrax 13

Ischyrolepis Steud. 19, 27, 42, **138**, **140**, 142, 179
  capensis (L.) Linder **128**, **143**, **32**(7), **36**(7), **37**(22)
  cincinnata (Mast.) Linder **130**, **138**, 139, 141, **27**(1), **30**(4), **34**(5), **36**(4)
  curviramis (Kunth.) Linder 139
  eleocharis (Mast.) Linder 141, **34**(7), **36**(2)
  gaudichaudiana (Kunth.) Linder 143
  ocreata (Kunth.) Linder 143
  paludosa (Pillans) Linder 141
  pratensis Esterhuysen 139
  sieberi (Kunth.) Linder **132**, **142**, **143**, 3, **38**(7)
  sporadica Esterhuysen 139

subverticellata Steud. **134**, **136**, 4, **36**(3), **38**(3, 4), 42, **140**, **172**, **173**
tenuissima (Kunth) Linder 141
triflora (Rottb.) Linder 143

Lyginia 18

Mastersiella Gilg-Ben. 10, 18, 19, 27, 42
  digitata (Thunb.) Gilg-Ben. **108**, 27, **33**(8), **36**(9), **40**(1)

Nevillea Esterhuysen & Linder 18, 19, 42
  obtusissima (Steud.) Linder **100**, **38**(1)
  singularis Esterhuysen 100

Orchidaceae 3

Oreotragus 13

Otomys 12

Platycaulos Linder 18, 19, 42
  compressus (Rottb.) Linder 158
  major (Mast.) Linder **158**, **32**(1), **40**(3)

Proteaceae 3

Restio Rottb. 11, 13, 18, 19, 23, 27, 42, 129, 150, 152, 154, 156
  ambiguus Mast. 153
  bifidus Thunb. **154**, 155, 12, **39**(21)
  bifurcus Nees ex Mast. **154**, **155**, **39**(22), 179
  communis Pillans 155
  dispar Mast. **146**, **156**, **157**, **37**(13), **40**(7)
  distichus Rottb. **156**, **157**
  dodii Pillans **156**, 157
  egregius Hochst.**144**, 153
  festuciformis Nees ex Mast. 11
  filiformis Poir. 155
  fourcadei Pillans 4
  leptostachyus Kunth 157
  micans Nees 153
  multiflorus Spreng 155

pedicellatus Mast. 151, 153
perplexus Kunth 153
quadratus Mast. 151, 172
quinquefarius Nees 150, 151, 8, 34(6), 36(6), 40(6)
sarocladus Mast. 157
sejunctus Mast. 153
tetragonus Thunb. 148, 150, 122, 151, 30(8), 172
triticeus Rottb. 157, 35(10)

Rhodocoma Nees 18, 18, 42
capensis Nees ex Steud. 92, 13, 170
fruticosa (Thunb.) Linder 90
gigantea (Kunth.) Linder 172, 173

Sedges 22, 23, 18

Staberoha Kunth 8, 9, 18, 19, 38(10, 11), 42, 88, 89
banksii Pillans 86, 88, 37(15, 16)
cernua (L. f.) Dur. & Schinz 88, 34(3, 4)
distachyos (Rottb.) Kunth 88
vaginata (Thunb.) Pillans 88

Tetraria thermalis 22

Thamnochortus Berg. 9, 18, 19, 41, 42, 29(3), 36(5), 75, 76, 78, 80, 82, 84, 39(24)
arenarius Esterhuysen 79, 85
cinereus Linder 165, 170

erectus (Thunb.) Mast. 83, 16
fraternus Pillans 81
fruticosus Berg. 83, 31(11), 162
gracilis Mast. 84, 85
guthrieae Pillans 80, 81, 85
insignis Mast. 82, 83, 11, 16, 39(25), 47, 166, 167, 172
levynsiae Pillans 85
lucens (Poir.) Linder 74, 79, 9, 30(3), 33(13), 35(12, 13), 38(12), 39(23), 41(16), 170
nutans (Thunb.) Pillans 81
obtusus Pillans 80, 81, 85
pellucidus Pillans 176, 166, 168
punctatus Pillans 78, 79
spicigerus (Thunb.) Spreng. 76, 83, 36(1)
sporadicus Pillans 78, 79, 85

Willdenowia Thunb. 10, 16, 18, 19, 26, 42, 106
affinis Pillans 107
glomerata (Thunb.) Linder 104, 106, 107, 35(11), 38(15), 40(8)
humilis Nees ex Mast. 106, 107
incurvata (Thunb.) Linder 106, 107 13, 31(10), 32(2), 33(10), 36(10)
sulcata Mast. 106, 107, 41(13)
teres Thunb. 106, 107, 39(20), 41(12, 15)

Notes

Notes

Els Dorrat Haaksma was born and educated in the Netherlands, where she graduated with a Doctorandus biology (M Sc) from the University of Utrecht, having done part of her post graduate studies at the University of Manchester in England. She then left for South Africa and settled in Johannesburg. After many years of teaching biology at high school level she worked as a senior tutor for the Academic Support Programme at the University of the Witwatersrand for seven years.

After moving to Cape Town in 1988 she spent three years doing research on the cytology of the Restionaceae at the University of Cape Town, before taking up the challenge of writing this book, in which she combined her love for botany, teaching and art.

She has three children and lives in the Marina da Gama.

Peter Linder has been working on the Restionaceae since 1981 and has published extensively on the family, dealing with the classification, dispersal mechanisms and pollination modes. His research has been backed up by extensive fieldwork in the Cape mountains as well as studies on the Australian Restionaceae. After completing his PhD at the University of Cape Town on the classification of the orchid genus *Disa* he worked at the National Botanical Institute and was posted to the Royal Botanic Gardens at Kew for three years. Since 1987 he has been a lecturer at the University of Cape Town.

ABOUT THE BOTANICAL SOCIETY

Founded in 1913 it is the mission of the Botanical Society of South Africa to win the hearts, minds and material support of individuals and organizations, wherever they may be, for the conservation, cultivation, study and wise use of the indigenous flora and vegetation of southern Africa.

ARE YOU A MEMBER?

If you are not already a member we invite you to join. The Society's branches around the country offer a wide range of activities such as hikes and botanical walks, illustrated lectures, tours and conservation activism. Members receive the colourful and informative quarterly magazine *Veld & Flora*, free admission to the eight Botanical Gardens and an annual selection of seed from Kirstenbosch.

By joining the Society you will be helping to protect South Africa's natural floral heritage – need your membership and support.

To join please contact:

The Membership Department
Botanical Society of South Africa
Private Bag X10
Claremont
7735
RSA

Telephone: (021) 797-2090
Fax: (021) 797-2376
e-mail: botsocsa@gem.co.za

or visit our website at
www.botanicalsociety.org.za